The
Freedom of God
and
Human Liberation

ALEXANDER J. McKELWAY

SCM PRESS
London

TRINITY PRESS INTERNATIONAL
Philadelphia

First published 1990

SCM Press
26–30 Tottenham Road
London N1 4BZ

Trinity Press International
3725 Chestnut Street
Philadelphia, PA 19104

British Library Cataloguing in Publication Data

McKelway, Alexander J.
The freedom of God and human liberation.
1. Christian doctrine. God
I. Title
231

ISBN 0–334–02466–8

Library of Congress Cataloging-in-Publication Data

McKelway, Alexander J.
The freedom of God and human liberation /
Alexander J. McKelway.
p. cm.
Includes bibliographical references and index.
ISBN 0–334–02466–8 (pbk.)
1. Liberty–Religious aspects–Christianity.   2. God.
I. Title.
BT810.2.M385   1990
231'.4–dc20   90–44867

Typeset at The Spartan Press Ltd, Lymington, Hants
and printed in Great Britain by
Clays Ltd, St Ives plc, Bungay Suffolk

CONTENTS

	Acknowledgments	vii
	Introduction	ix
1	Recovering the Freedom of God	1
2	The Structure of Divine Freedom	17
3	Thinking about God	33
4	The Liberating Word	53
5	Liberating Theology	69
6	Revolutionary Freedom	88
	Notes	104
	Index	120

For Paul Lehmann

ACKNOWLEDGMENTS

The chapters presented in this book are based upon the Warfield Lectures delivered at Princeton Theological Seminary in the fall of 1987, and I wish here to thank Professor David Willis, President Thomas Gillespie, and other faculty colleagues at Princeton for the invitation to take part in that distinguished lectureship.

No one produces a book — not even one as brief as this — without help. Among my colleagues at Davidson, I am grateful to Karl Plank for useful comments on the text of the lectures, and to Frank Bliss for a most careful and comprehensive editing of the publishers' proofs. Special thanks are due to Philip Lee, of the Church of St Stephen and St John in Saint John, New Brunswick, and Wallace Alston, of the Nassau Presbyterian Church in Princeton, New Jersey, for undertaking substantive reviews of the book manuscript. The observations and suggestions offered by these two scholarly pastors were invaluable. Virginia Hall Bowman prepared the index with her usual thoroughness and Harold Rast of Trinity Press International, together with the editors of SCM Press, managed the production of this book with remarkable dispatch. I am grateful for the help of all these colleagues and friends and assure the reader that any remaining errors of fact, judgment, and style are mine and not theirs.

My use of, and enthusiasm for, the theology of Karl Barth is everywhere apparent in this book and requires no special acknowledgment. I nevertheless offer it in an effort to counteract the tedious *ressentiment* that has made the word "Barthian" an epithet in American theology and obscured the continuing importance of Barth's thought for the life of the church. Less obvious, but no less important, is the influence of Paul Lehmann, who, more than any other American theologian, through his life, teaching and writing, has held up the two principles which inform these pages: the freedom of God *and* human liberation. In gratitude for his leadership and continuing friendship, this book is dedicated to him.

INTRODUCTION

In the Soviet Union a "new thinking" (*novoe myshlenie*) and "openness" (*glasnost*) has made possible a radical turn toward economic and political freedom after decades of stagnation and decline. Given the stagnation of Western Christianity over the same decades, its failure effectively to further the cause of liberation or stop the decline of its influence, the question must arise as to whether the church, too, is not in need of "new thinking". This book is driven by the conviction that the manifest failure of the church in our time in large measure is due to its neglect of the freedom of God, that is, the unique and independent reality of God. As liberals and conservatives, progressives and reactionaries, we all tend to think of God in terms of our own values and to project upon the divine will our own intellectual and social agendas. We need, a "new thinking" that thinks of God as *God*, as free in himself, and we need a new "openness" to the variety of ways that such a God can inspire and enable true liberation.

The approach to the freedom of God and human liberation taken in these six chapters proceeds in the following way. (1) After establishing the need to recover the freedom of God for the sake of human liberation, I note several unsuccessful attempts to do so, and then make a first probe into the inner nature of God's freedom which finds expression in God's living and acting in love. (2) The life and activity of God reveals a four-fold structure of freedom which I apply in each of its four aspects to the struggle for liberation. (3) Since the freedom of God requires a new conceptualizing of God, I examine some of the problems involved in authentic thought about God and propose a "meta-critical" thinking appropriate both for the inconceivable nature of God and for the conceivable nature of faith. (4) As the liberating word of a free God, the Bible has a freedom whose structure corresponds to God's freedom. Here I attempt to show the significance of the freedom of the word (which includes its humanity, its self-authentication and self-interpretation) for the cause of liberation. (5) A theo-logy which is really a "word" about a "God" who is free, must itself be free and liberating. This claim requires a consideration of the present state of theology and the extent to which it may itself need liberating for more faithful and courageous service. (6) I conclude by discussing the nature of human freedom, which is the goal of the freedom of God. We reach the conclusion that God's freedom is revolutionary in a way that radically surpasses all human revolutions, and that human freedom is found in obedience to God's liberating activity — and not in the closed and hopeless circle of human autonomy.

These assertions give rise to a vast number of theological questions, a few of which were raised by representatives of liberation theology when these chapters were presented as lectures. Since it is especially from that side that we would like to be understood, it may be appropriate to address a few of those questions in this introduction.

In the first chapter, "Recovering the freedom of God," I argue that the transcendent "otherness" of God is essential for the cause of freedom. The question has been asked whether the emphasis should not be on the incarnational presence of God, since the ground and hope of human liberation are seen most clearly in the love, power, and justice of God made visible in Jesus Christ. While liberation theology is right in maintaining the centrality of Christ, its Christology emphasis is often one-sided. A "Christology from below" (Sobrino, Gutiérrez, etc.) correctly discovers in the life of Jesus a warrant and model for social change, but if liberation theology does not also view Jesus "from above," it misses the divinity which alone makes Christ the liberator. Jesus constantly pointed away from himself to that "other" — as if to remind us that the human form of God *pro nobis* cannot be understood apart from the nature of God as he is in himself.

When attention to the transcendent otherness of God does not accompany Christological reflection, the result must inevitably be a theology of divine immanence in which the life of God incarnate is confused with our life, his cause with our causes, and his saving activity with the ambiguities of human revolution and reaction. This confusion is apparent, it seems to me, in Peter C. Hodgson's *New Birth of Freedom: A Theology of Bondage and*

Liberation,[1] and in his *God in History: Shapes of Human Freedom*.[2] Among significant theological studies of liberation in the last several decades (Moltmann's *Crucified God*, Käsemann's *Jesus Means Freedom*, Pannenberg's *The Idea of God and Human Freedom*) Hodgson's work presents the most detailed investigation of the meaning of freedom from both a philosophical and theological perspective. His exploration of the structure of freedom in many ways breaks new ground,[3] and his conclusion that human freedom is non-autonomous coincides with my own. Hodgson wants to maintain that our freedom is defined and authorized by Jesus, whose resurrection is the ultimate source of liberation. He can even say that this "liberating power . . . is defined by reference to God. Such power is not immanent and humanistic, the self-generating and self-emancipating historical potentiality of the human species; rather it is the power of *God*, who is the *Lord* of history, the *Creator* of the heavens and the earth."[4]

The trouble is, that Hodgson places these assertions toward the end of his first book, having earlier suspended the question of the existence of a "transcendent liberating power" while he undertook a phenomenological investigation of freedom. We should want to place such a reference to the "God who is the Lord" at the beginning, as a necessary axiom of faith without which the character and hope of human freedom cannot be examined. Furthermore, it is difficult to take at face value Hodgson's assurance that the liberating power of God is not "immanent", nor "the historical potentiality of the human species", since he quite clearly adopts Hegel's view of the identity of God and history. "[T]he actual working of [God's] government . . . is the history of the world."[5] and . . . "'God' and 'history' are essentially co-constitutive categories . . ."[6] The freedom of God cannot be bracketed and set aside while we otherwise determine the nature of freedom and its possibilities, nor can we agree to any assertion of divine immanence, for that condemns the human prospect to Nietzsche's "eternal recurrence of the same."

When God is identified with human history (which is the significant activity of any nation, class, race, or sex), or with any particular political or ethical system, the result must be the reduplication of ideologies which are powerless to achieve human liberation, and may actually contribute to oppression. A theology dedicated to the liberating power and grace of God must therefore recover a sense of God as "God," as radically "other" and free in himself, as a God who acts, lives and loves in freedom.

Another question has been raised concerning "The Structure of Divine Freedom" presented in the second chapter. There God's freedom is described in terms of a four-fold structure. God is free (*a*) *in* himself, (*b*) *from* all other being, (*c*) *for* his creation, and even (*d*) *from* his ways of being free *for* us. Each of these freedoms is an extension of the primary freedom within the trinitarian life of God and each holds special meaning for the cause of human liberation. For instance, God's freedom from other being means that God does not belong to the nexus of political cause and effect, and is therefore free to redeem the oppressive consequences of both revolution and reaction. God's freedom from any particular way of his being for us means, among other things, that theology cannot be absolutistic in its understanding of the divine will, but must be open to ever new (and often surprising) expressions of the liberating activity of God.

Against this latter claim, the objection has been raised that such an openness must produce an enervating uncertainty in which actual opportunities for liberation are abandoned in favor of remote possibilities. It is true that reflection can be an excuse for inaction, but it is equally true that a premature identification of God's will both with democratic capitalism and with Marxism has rendered theologians on the political right and on the left incapable of responding to unexpected developments in the struggle for liberation. The assumption that American democracy best approximates the freedom of God, made it impossible for conservatives to imagine free elections under the Sandinista government in Nicaragua, just as the identification of socialist justice with God's justice made it impossible for liberals to imagine the dissolution of Soviet communism in favor of free markets and free elections. Those in the middle, whom we might call "liberal democrats," may find that even their ideals do not necessarily represent what, in the providence of God, may serve freedom best. Our expectations concerning the democratization of formerly communist societies may not coincide with the reality of the situation. Stephen Sestanovich notes that in the Soviet Union, "the freedom to speak up, organize, and assemble may present itself primarily as a long-sought opportunity to fight things out . . . To be a liberal is in effect to encourage the escalation of conflicts that could before long tear the USSR apart."[7] To participate in the ever-changing shape and direction of liberation praxis, theology must be open to the infinite variety of ways that God's freedom for human life takes place.

Because this essay, especially in the second and third chapters, makes reflection upon the freedom of God a prerequisite for liberation theology, it has been criticized for reversing the order of "praxis and *then* reflection." Derived from Marx's second thesis on Feuerbach ("Truth resides not in contemplation, but in action"), [8] the principle of praxis over reflection has become axiomatic for most liberation theologians. According to Dorothee Soelle, "[T]he verification principle of every theological statement is the praxis that it enables for the future. Theological statements contain as much truth as they deliver practically in transforming reality."[9] Similarly, Gustavo Gutiérrez speaks of "theology as critical reflection on praxis."[10] In this essay we take the opposite view: authentic thought about God (God as free in himself, God as *God*), is a necessary precondition for any liberating praxis.

The principle of praxis over reflection carries with it two distinct disadvantages. *First,* apart from its being self-consuming (the priority of praxis over reflection being itself a product of reflection), this principle has served to immunize liberation theology from critical appraisal and correction. For example, Leonardo and Clodovis Boff argue that "criticism made of liberation theology by those who judge it on a purely conceptual level" is "radically irrelevant" unless the critic can answer satisfactorily the question: "What part have *you* played in the effective and integral liberation of the oppressed?"[11] Among some representatives of Black and feminist theologies critical questions are disallowed from any who are not themselves members of the oppressed race or sex. Such privileged argumentation does injury to movements for liberation, because it isolates them in an intellectual ghetto where there is no possibility of constructive criticism. Insofar as such argumentation signals a sense of moral privilege, it betrays the freedom it espouses by imposing a social works-righteousness upon the science of theology. A truly liberating theology cannot be pelagian: it will not turn again to the bondage of law, or "submit again to [that] yoke of slavery" (Gal. 5:1).

Second, when praxis takes priority over reflection one can become blind to ideological commitments made in the heat of action. Such commitments can easily displace faith as the source and norm of liberation effort. For instance, some caught up in the fervor of nationalism could create a "German-Church" or an "American civil-religion," while others involved in social, racial and sexual struggles produced a Marxist-, Black-, or feminist-theology. These "happy little hyphens" (Barth) impose upon the work of theology ideological commitments which are alien to its task and are the result of a failure to reflect upon the freedom of God — which freedom is greater than that promised by any of those ideologies. Just as faith without works is dead, so theology is irrelevant without some sort of engagement of the theologian in the struggle for human freedom. This does not mean, however, that action takes precedence over thought, or is superior to it. Hanna Arendt, commenting upon the *vita activa*, has noted that "[T]he concern underlying all its activities is not the same as and is neither superior nor inferior to the central concern of the *vita contemplativa*."[12]

Finally, some have protested the gender specific references to God made in the lectures upon which these chapters are based. Such objections came as no surprise, since a prohibition against male pronominal reference to God has become *de rigueur* in most North American seminaries and divinity schools. That this new regulation of theological language has been put in place on strictly social and stylistic grounds without serious theological debate is a cause of wonder. I have been careful here to keep references to persons inclusive. Moreover, I admit in chapter four that gender references to God in scripture and tradition are a product of the accidental fact of history that men were in control of religious discourse when those authorities were produced. I also argue, however, that the Bible's text, although fraught with every imaginable prejudice, nonetheless contains a self-critical dimension that denies that God is male, or has anything to do with male presumption and pride.

The problematic nature of biblical and theological language notwithstanding, in this book the pronouns "he," "him," and "his" are used in reference to God, although I have attempted to mitigate such usage. These pronouns (as well as other gender specific references to God) are employed for two reasons. First, in a sustained discussion of the divine nature, constant avoidance of pronouns is not only stylistically awkward, but tends to depersonalize the image of God. This latter danger is already at hand in a discussion which emphasizes the "otherness" of God. Second, and more importantly, the elimination of male pronouns for God, or the substitution of female pronouns, compounds the very theological error which those tactics intend to correct. Such methods suggest that the problem is an inequality in religious language, which is at once both cause and effect of a pervasive sexual inequality. The assumption seems to be that, when speaking of God, we properly model divinity after our humanity, and must, therefore, be inclusive in doing so. To avoid projecting human images upon the divine, some have employed various neuter references to God, but insofar as such non-gender ways of speaking of God are the result of a desire for either the amalgamation of *or* the mutual exclusion of male and female humanity, they, too, are projections of the various rejections and resentments that belong to our self-image.

The thesis of this book is that the freedom and *otherness* of God empowers and inspires human liberation. It would, therefore, be a contradiction to adopt any of the current strategies for manipulating God-language, for they all perpetuate the theological error of projecting upon the divine the highly problematic nature of our own self-consciousness. We simply have to understand that the Bible's personal imagery for God directs us to a reality quite different from our own. Unless this is understood, the way in which the "fatherhood" and "lordship" of God can redeem and transform the ambiguities of human love, power, and justice will be missed. Neither the "fatherhood" nor "lordship" of God has anything to do with the sorry history of male presumption — except to call it into radical question and judgment. The point is not to avoid the Bible's way of speaking of God, but to employ that language with theological understanding.

Notes

1. Peter C. Hodgson, *New Birth of Freedom: A theology of Bondage and Liberation*, (Philadelphia, Fortress Press, 1976).

2. Peter C. Hodgson, *God in History: Shapes of Human Freedom* (Nashville, Abingdon Press, 1989).

3. Hodgson, 1976, 105ff.

4. Hodgson, 1976, 291.

5. Hodgson, 1976, 270.

6. Hodgson, 1989, 44.

7. Stephen Sestanovich, "Responses to Fukuyama," *The National Interest,* Summer 1989, 33.

8. Alasdair C. MacIntyre, *Marxism and Christianity* (Notre Dame, University of Notre Dame Press, 1968), 59.

9. Dorothee Soelle, *Political Theology* (Philadelphia, Fortress Press, 1974), 76.

10. Gustavo Gutiérrez, *A Theology of Liberation* (Maryknoll, Orbis Books, 1973), 6.

11. Leonardo and Clodovis Boff, *Introduction to Liberation Theology* (Maryknoll, Orbis Books, 1988), 9.

12. Hanna Arendt, *The Human Condition* (Chicago, University of Chicago Press, 1958), 17.

1

Recovering the Freedom of God

Introduction

A. *The theme*

The juxtaposition of the "the freedom of God" and "human liberation" must appear unconventional, because when applying theology to human concerns, especially to the momentous issue of liberation, we usually refer to the human face of God, to God's solidarity with humanity, and not to the transcendence and otherness of God — the way God is free in himself.

In this book, however, I will argue that the freedom of God is indispensable for any theology which attempts to address the human condition. Too often in the theology, worship, and programs of the church God is identified with our own interests and commitments. Thus the Christian community deprives itself of the confidence and hope which only faith in a God who is really "God" can bring. This point becomes all the more important where the church undertakes the cause of Christ in the struggle for freedom. Here, especially, it is essential that the God to whom the oppressed turn for help not be a mere projection of human ideals and judgments, but the God who is *God*, and therefore really able to deliver his people from bondage. Theology can perform no greater service today than to lift up the reality and power of God in the cause of justice and peace.

The Bible makes clear that God cares about the oppressed. Amos preached against those who "buy the poor for silver and the needy for a pair of shoes" (Amos 8:6),[1] and the Word made flesh "proclaim(ed) release to the captives" (Luke 4:18). Thus we are both assured and warned by Karl Barth that

God always takes his stand unconditionally and passionately

on this side and on this side alone: against the lofty and on behalf of the lowly, against those who already enjoy right and privilege and on behalf of those who are denied it and deprived of it.[2]

Theologies of liberation have responded to this truth by taking the side of God against political oppression in Latin America and South Africa, against racism in the United States, against the global fact of sexism, and against a growing number of other oppressions. In doing so they have overcome centuries of Christian quietism by insisting that political action is a necessary correlate of faith. For liberation theology, the cause of freedom does not constitute one among other imperatives of Christian faith, but is a concern fundamental to the whole.[3] Every aspect of faith includes the liberating activity of God and requires of women and men of faith obedient participation in that activity. In a world whose survival depends upon the pursuit of peace and justice, liberation theology must be seen as a particularly timely gift of God to the church — and it ought to elicit from the church not only thankfulness and solidarity, but also the best critical reflection that can be placed at its disposal.

Today critical reflection upon the relation between theology and freedom is especially important in light of the current swift evolution of soviet and Eastern European societies from Marxism–Leninism to democracy. The liberation of those societies from an oppressive and stultifying communism is certainly welcomed. There is, however, a danger. Freedom from state control has allowed the release of barely suppressed anti-Semitism in Russia, violence against Christians in Azerbaijan and Muslims in Armenia, and ethnic conflict in Romania. Furthermore, the movement to a free market in Eastern Europe may lead to unemployment and a duplication of the injustices attendant to laissez faire capitalism, and the clamor for independence may result in the Balkanization of soviet and Eastern European states. If these and other dangers are to be avoided, a vision of the nature and source of human freedom quite different from that taught by the free-market democracies must guide these newly liberated peoples. Here the church may be of service if it can hold up the freedom of God as the source of liberation, and obedience to that God as requisite for real freedom.

Thus this book takes up the theme of the freedom of God as it relates to the struggle for human liberation. More specifically, there is here an attempt to recover for the cause of liberation a neglected dimension in contemporary theology, that is, a sense of the transcendent, objective reality of God, which has been termed the freedom of God *a se*, "in himself." Without this dimension, the meaning of God *pro nobis*, "for us," cannot be understood or effect real liberation.

B. *The question of Christology*

Before proceeding further, a question must be faced. Is it useful in the struggle for liberation to focus upon the mystery of God's transcendent otherness? Do not the practical concerns of life direct us to the concrete expression of God's will revealed in Christ, rather than to abstract conceptions of God's transcendent being? Calvin cautions us against undue emphasis upon the mystery of the divine being. In commenting upon the passage ("The Lord, the Lord, merciful and gracious"),[4] he wrote:

> [God's] powers are mentioned, by which he is shown to us not as he is in himself, but as he is toward us: so that the recognition of him consists more in living experience than in vain and high-flown speculation.[5]

Barth's theology also rejected a speculative approach to God's nature and moved steadily through the *Church Dogmatics* toward a "christocentricity." Neither Calvin nor Barth considered it legitimate to address the freedom of God apart from his freedom for us in Jesus Christ.

In light of these considerations, is it legitimate to focus on the inner rather than incarnational nature of God? There are two answers to this question. First, it must be admitted that there is no knowledge of God's mysterious otherness and freedom except through the revelation of Jesus Christ. Barth once wrote, "There is no greater depth in God's being and work than that revealed . . . under this name."[6] Notwithstanding the correctness of this statement, we must also say that the incarnate Christ points away from the person of Jesus to the reality and nature of God. "Why do you ask me about what is good? One there is who is good" (Matt. 19:17). "He who believes in me, believes not in me, but in him who sent me" (John 12:44). Just because it is God whois revealed in Jesus Christ, we are directed by Christ himself to keep before us the transcendent reality of God.[7]

Second, even if the logic of Christology did not direct theological attention toward the divine nature itself, the present cultural-religious situation would. In many ways the church today is faced with the problem with which Barth began. The desire to identify God with national ideals, so obvious in the German Christian Church under Hitler, has been visible all along in American civil religion. Oliver North made this clear during the Iran-Contra hearings by constantly evoking God's name in support of the Reagan administration's violence against the Nicaraguan people. This same projection of self-interest upon the image of God, always prevalent in American evangelism, has in recent years achieved some sort of apogee in Oral Roberts's announcement of his return from the dead to "reign beside Jesus."[8] From a different direction the same presumption appears in Carol Christ's approval of the claim of one writer that, as a woman, she had found God in herself "and loved her fiercely."[9] Such illustrations abound in contemporary culture and indicate the need in the church today for a recovery of the independent reality and freedom of God.

c. *The relevance of God's freedom*

What can a recovery of the freedom of God offer to the cause of freedom? An answer to that question will emerge in the course of this essay, but the following may serve as preliminary illustration. Liberation theology rightly insists that the God who is for us is against the oppressor and identifies with his or her (one might better say *our*) victims. Thus there is no reason to complain if the theologies represented by James Cone, Rosemary Ruether, and Gustavo Gutiérrez pronounce God's judgment (respectively) upon whites, males, and the affluent, and identify the cause of God (again respectively) with blacks, women, and the poor. A problem arises, however, when new liberation theologies expand the list of oppressors and oppressed to include North Americans and Indians, management and labor, industrial and aboriginal societies, adults and children, hetero- and homosexuals, and the like.[10] A confusing mix of charge and countercharge removes the solidarity required of those who serve the revolutionary justice of God and threatens the possibility of human community, which forms the context of freedom.

Too often a narrow and self-serving view of freedom intrudes upon the struggle for liberation. Pursuing their own economic interests, Romanian miners helped crush public protest against an oppressive government, and regional calls for independence threaten the progress toward democracy in the Soviet Union. As they seek to participate in the cause of justice, Christians ought not to make a similar mistake and believe themselves in possession of God's judgment and advocacy, *uncritically* applying these to their own cause. We forget that first of all it is *God's* freedom with which we have to do and upon which true liberation depends. The Christian community needs to recognize that God is "God," that we cannot identify God with our own causes and strategies, that in respect to God's justice we all stand under both judgment and grace. If the struggle for liberation is to move beyond self-interest to solidarity under God, it must have a sense of the prior and indispensable self- sufficiency, independence, and power of God as he is in himself.

Having introduced the theme of the freedom of God, we can move forward by doing two things. First, we must consider the problem of abstract and personal projections of God, and then begin an investigation of the transcendent freedom of God by examining the primary characteristics of the inner being of God as action and love.

I. The Co-optation of "God" in Theology: Some Historical Examples

The cause of liberation is badly served when theology neglects the freedom of God and uncritically identifies God with human will, intention, and judgment. In light of Barth's uncontestable assertion that "in our weakness" we make of God "a puny little idol,"[11] how is this to be avoided?

One answer has been the attempt to preserve the transcendence of God by way of philosophical abstraction. Neoplatonic theologians, like the Pseudo-Dionysius and a contemporary representative, Paul Tillich, conceived of God as "pure being" or "being-itself." For the Pseudo-Dionysius, God is "unpredicated" and alternately "darkness above light" and "unapproachable light"; Tillich regularly speaks of God as the "ground" or "power of being."[12] Tillich, for instance, believed that by employing such conceptions he could avoid the self-projection inherent in super-naturalism and direct theological attention to the "God above God," that is, the God above the god of theism.[13] This approach, however, offers no protection from anthropological projection, because the distinction between the divine and human collapses when the content and character of "God" is conceived in terms either of the negation or perfection of aspects of human being. The evacuation of all predication from God attempted by the Pseudo-Dionysius represents the projection of a perennial self-negation which believes that "All transitory things are but a parable."[14] On the other hand, the perfection of human qualities may be seen in Plotinus's understanding of God as "truth itself," "beauty itself," "justice itself," or as the unity of the finite polarities of human being suggested by Tillich: "subjectivity/objectivity," "dynamics/form," and "freedom/destiny."[15]

A similar attempt to guard the divine being against anthropological projection can be seen in Thomas Aquinas, who argued that an objective knowledge of God is possible on the basis of certain evidences in the world of nature. Once again, the knowledge of God Aquinas claimed apart from and prior to revelation is, in fact, an abstraction from the hopes and conditions of human existence. Aquinas's concept of a "prime mover" or a "first cause" may easily be seen as the projection of the activity and dynamic of human life which desires ultimate significance and status. Similarly, his notion of God as "necessary being" reflects the human desire to escape contingency, and his definition of God as "maximum being" and "universal designer" are expressions of what we would like to say about our values and science, but cannot without recourse to the idea of deity. Long ago Feuerbach observed that "the object of any subject is nothing else than the subject's own nature taken objectively," and that "the mystery of the inexhaustible fullness of the divine predicates is therefore nothing else than the mystery of human nature considered as an infinitely varied, infinitely modifiable, but, consequently, phenomenal being."[16]

In the fifteenth century Nicholas of Cusa tried to maintain a radical distinction between God and human being by way of a "negative theology." It is enough, he taught, to know that God is infinite (*not* finite), immutable (*not* subject to change), invisible, etc.[17] As penitential and corrective theology, the "learned ignorance" of Cusa has its place. It was used in altered form by the early Barth, whose own negative theology of the "otherness" and "unknowableness" of God was directed against liberalism's identification of God and humanity. But theology cannot rest in a *via negativa*, because an "unknown God" who *remains* unknown is not, according to Paul's speech in Acts 17, the God revealed in Jesus Christ. The "infinite" is not the God who wills to reveal himself to us by being for us. Furthermore, the God of the *via negativa* must also be exposed as an expression of our own humanity — to the extent that it betrays a universal desire to escape the limitation of human nature by projecting from it an *unlimited* being of its own construction.

Late in the eighteenth century Schleiermacher wanted to correct the misappropriation of God he saw in both pietism and orthodoxy, and therefore sought a more valid conception of God in the depths of religious consciousness. For Schleiermacher, "the finding of oneself in immediate self-consciousness as absolutely dependent is . . . the only way that, in general, our own being and the infinite being of God can be one."[18] Here God is not only the ground of all religion, but is at the same time the ulterior ground of our whole self-consciousness — the mysterious center of our intelligent and active existence. It is difficult to avoid the view that Schleiermacher's theology has to do not so much with the objective reality of God as with our "own subjective aspirations, fears, and ideals as they become objectified in theological ideas and institutions."[19] In this conception of God, Schleiermacher appears unwittingly to duplicate the approach of Kant, who abstracted God from the universal moral imperative as a necessary presupposition of the lawgiver and guarantor of practical reason. "The postulate of the possibility of a highest derived good (the best world) is at the same time the postulate of the reality of a highest original good, namely, the existence of God."[20] Nor in this respect does Schleiermacher seem far from his old nemesis, Hegel, whose concept of God was a forceful and profound description of the movement of nature and spirit which proceeds from ourselves and returns to ourselves. Hegel's God is, finally, "the process of life itself."[21] "Man knows God only insofar as God knows himself in man. This knowledge is God's self-consciousness but also God's knowledge of man. God's knowledge of man is also man's knowledge of God. The spirit of man which is to know God is only the spirit of God himself."[22] Later, even Albrecht Ritschl, who thought he possessed a more objective view of God, could write that "God is the power, which man worships, which upholds his worth," or again, "We know the nature of God and Christ only in their worth for us."[23]

Such conceptions of God appear to derive more from self-abstraction than from the concrete disclosure of God in Christ. Thus they offer no defense against an uncritical identification of human being with God, or of human values and programs with the freedom of God. If, however, the transcendent reality of God cannot be protected by abstraction, neither can it be secured by avoiding anthropomorphic references to God. Against the speculative-philosophical categories of Thomism and nominalism, Luther insisted upon very human language and concepts of God. Of the Nicene term *homoousia*, Luther once admitted that he "hated this word and . . . refused to use it."[24] For Luther, God is identified with the babe in the manger, the carpenter's son, the real man who sat at table, settled domestic disputes, stands at the door and knocks, and who died on a cross *pro nobis*.[25] Calvin, too, had a strong sense of the humanity of a God who, as he always put it, "accommodates" himself to human frailty. So there is every reason to welcome the tendency of contemporary theology to associate God in Christ with such personal terms as "friend," "companion," or even "partner."[26]

There is thus no reason to avoid personal-anthropomorphic language about God in the church, but care must be taken that the use of such language contains a dialectical acknowledgment of the transcendence of God. Reformation theology included that acknowledgment. Luther found in the cross the ultimate expression of God's solidarity with us, but in that most human event he never forgot the unimaginable otherness of God — upon which "we gaze with blinded eyes like a mole."[27] Luther avoided the error of collapsing the suffering of God into our suffering, making it a mere empathetic identification with the human condition. Nor did he confuse the justification accomplished on the cross with our justice. Here, supremely, Luther's sense of the freedom of God achieved a revolutionary breakthrough. Where once the justice and righteousness of God had been understood in the medieval church as an extension of natural law and jurisprudence, Luther recognized in the cross a quite different justice and "rightness" which belongs to the freedom of God in himself. God's justice is "divine ignorance and free forgiveness of sins."[28] For Luther, the justice of God is not only other than, but is radically contradictory to, all human concepts of justice and rightness — even contradictory to our sense of reality.

> There is in me sin, unrighteousness and horror of death. Yet I must look elsewhere and see no sin. This is wonderful, not to see what I see, not to feel what I feel. Before my eyes I see a gulden, or a sword, or a fire, and I must say "There is no gulden, no sword, no fire." The forgiveness of sins is like that.[29]

In God's justice the wrong are made right and the unjust, just.

The question is not whether a theology employs extensive human imagery for God. The question is whether such a theology keeps in view the freedom of God — a freedom which is never exhausted or encircled by human thought. Such a view of the freedom of God functions as a constant corrective to all theology and discloses ever new possibilities for liberty and hope.

When the issue is put this way, we cannot avoid noticing a counter tendency in contemporary theology, typified by Gordon Kaufman's *Theology for a Nuclear Age.*[30] For Kaufman, the real possibility of global self-annihilation presents modern culture with the fact of a human rather than divine sovereignty over the world. This fact, he believes, requires a theology which abandons notions of dominion, whether divine or human, eschews all claims of authority attached to religious texts, understands God as a symbol of the *telos* of evolutionary process, and views Christ as the example of love which alone gives promise for human community and survival. Kaufman's humanization of God in the service of an ecologically responsible theology in some respects reflects a proper sense of the being of God for us in the world. A problem arises, however, when he rejects the freedom of God to *be* God apart from human thought and historical process. Such a view renders God indistinguishable from human being. Kaufman's claim that our humanity, in the sovereign splendor of its best wisdom and most benevolent intention, is sufficient to rescue itself from a threat produced precisely *by* its best wisdom

and intention, appears unrealistic and naive. An effective "theology for a nuclear age" must bring to bear upon the manifest
failure of human possibility the divine possibility of deliverance
and hope.

"Theology," Kaufman writes, "should be judged in terms of
the adequacy with which it is fulfilling the objectives we humans
set for it."[31] This same insistence that theology conform to a
particular group's values can be found on the left when Juan Luis
Segundo asserts that a Marxist analysis of society constitutes a
necessary "pre-understanding" of the biblical text.[32] In other
words, theology must express *our* values. Such a view appears
also to dominate the religious right insofar as the objectives of
American foreign policy dictate the direction and content of its
theology.[33] When from the left or the right the church allows its
own or someone else's objectives to dictate the content of its
theology, when it does not take into account the prior freedom of
God in himself, it loses the self-critical perspective which is
necessary if movements for human liberation are to be delivered
from their own tragic limitations. On this issue we may find
better guidance from Allan Boesak, who warns that a liberating
theology "must not yield to uncritical accommodation, being a
'cultural theology' or a religion of culture."[34]

Any theology, whether conservative or liberal, whether reactionary, revolutionary, or revisionist, that so identifies the will of
God with human values that it measures itself against its own
objectives rather than against the free word of God, must
inevitably reproduce the human presumption that lies at the base
of every oppression. For this reason both conservative and
revolutionary theologies need the corrective of the freedom of
God.

If ideological projection intrudes so universally upon theology,
what can save our present project from the same fate? On what
grounds could it be claimed that a theology opened to the
freedom of God is any less liable to such projection? In answer, it
has to be admitted that, on the one hand, no human language or
thought about God can transcend the limitations of one's
historical, political, and sexual situation. Even if theology is
constantly on guard against the intrusion of ideological presuppositions, they will nonetheless work upon it without the
theologian being wholly conscious of their influence. On the

other hand, the impact of ideology upon theology can be mitigated by the critical perspective we are here attempting. In chapter 3 we will explore this issue in terms of the possibility of a "meta-critical" movement in which not only thought about God, but the thinker as well, is called into question and brought to the critical juncture of a divine self-disclosure which alone authenticates thought and speech about God.

Having introduced the idea of the prior, transcendent, and absolute freedom of God and having attempted, in a preliminary way, to show the need for this concept in contemporary theology, it is now necessary to undertake a more precise understanding of the freedom of God in preparation for its application in subsequent chapters.

II. The Freedom of God: Preliminary Definitions

Christ himself directs attention to the transcendence of God. In the existence of the man Jesus, God discloses his solidarity with female and male humanity, but because it is *God* who is there revealed, we are at the same time encountered by one who can never be uncritically identified with our way of being human. God stands over against our way of being human ultimately and absolutely. Although in Christ women and men are addressed by one who wills to be known as a person, who calls us into a personal relationship and thereby provides us with the possibility of being truly human persons, because it is *God* who does this, we are at the same time confronted by the mystery of the divine being, who as Paul Tillich reminds us again and again, is never just "*a* person, [but] the ground of everything personal."[35] God has so revealed himself in Christ that we are obliged to think of "him" as "Father," but God is not primarily "our" father, he is the Father of the Son, from whom both the Son and the Spirit proceed. Thus the father–name of God does not ask us to contemplate paternity or masculinity, but rather to reflect upon the Trinity and the fact that it is *God* who in wondrous transcendence decided in his absolute freedom and grace from all eternity to be for us in these three ways.[36]

A. *God as "God"*

According to Eberhard Busch, the primary dictum of Barth's

theology is the claim that "God is *God*."[37] This phrase, which probably originated with John of Damascus ("We cannot say what God is . . . only that God is God"), represented for Barth the fundamental and irreducible theological claim that God *is*. The tautology "God is God" is in fact the first step necessary "to avoid the equating of God [with] our concepts of God."[38] If faith must confess before any other thought simply that "God is," it must immediately be said that the claim "God is" does not mean that God "exists" as other things exist. This was what Paul Tillich meant when he denied the "existence" of God — and on this point he and Barth were in agreement. But Tillich believed that to say that "God is" means that God, as being-itself, participates in a reality of being which is common to God and all other things. "Everything participates in being-itself."[39] This Barth would not allow. That God "is" did not mean for him that "being" is, so to speak, the common denominator between the creator and the creature; rather, "God *is*" means that "God is *God*," or better, we should say, "God is *as* God."

In this investigation of the primary freedom of God as *God*, we begin with the simple but necessary assertion that "God is," and that "God is *as* God is." The circularity of this formula cannot be denied, but it is not an empty circle into which we are invited to place either abstract or concrete projections of ourselves. The content of that circle is provided by God's self-revelation, which discloses the two primary characteristics belonging to the way "God is God," namely, that God is God as one who acts — and who acts in love.[40]

B. *God as one who acts*

The statement that "God is as God" merely gives theological expression to the crucial formula of Exod. 3:14, "I am Yahweh" or "I am who I am." The scope of this discussion does not allow a review of the rich variety of interpretations of the word "Yahweh" — itself a peculiar combination of the first and third person singular of the Hebrew verb *haya* ("to be"). Suffice it to note that most Old Testament scholars place the verb-noun "Yahweh" in the active voice, rendering the term "I will be who I will be."[41] It is as if God were saying, "if you want to know who 'I am,' just watch!" So if we ask *how* God is as God, the first answer must be that God is a God who *acts*. Scripture portrays God as active, not passive. Indeed, our need to know something about the way God is *as* God antecedent to the way God is for us would be doomed from the start if we thought that tucked away in scripture there were also images, ideas, and concepts of God as a being quiet and dormant in the recesses of his own transcendent and absolute nature. The Bible knows no such God; it knows only a God who broods, speaks, creates, plants, judges, condemns, destroys, saves, etc.

In a way consistent with this biblical view of God, the medieval schoolmen spoke of God as *actus purus*, as "pure act" or actuality.[42] Theology can place no restraint upon the actualization of God's potentialities. Even where God withholds action (of judgment, rescue etc.), God's inactivity is a function of a sovereign deciding and willing. The concept of God's being in action is fundamental because it serves as a prohibition against the notion that here and there among the interstices of creation human destiny might become subject to some other decision, will, or action other than that of God. Concerning the cause of his people, their poverty and oppression, the God of Israel "neither slumbers nor sleeps."

God's being in action requires that we also speak of God as *living*. As the supremely living one, God gives life and opposes everything that threatens it. Now, obviously, the God who appeared to Moses as one who acts and lives cannot be thought of other than as *person*. God lives as an "I," and thus one must always speak of God as personal. It is a commonplace in modern theology (Buber, Brunner) to say that there can be no "I" without a "thou." That formula should not be taken to mean, however, that God, to be an "I," requires the creature as a thou.[43] In another rare point of agreement, both Barth and Tillich locate God's being as person in the trinitarian dynamic of the divine life. For Tillich the movement of God out of himself in the Son and back to himself in the Spirit provides the give and take of personal relationality in the eternal being of God.[44] Barth, on the other hand, sees an original and eternal relationality within the triune being of God that provides the basis for the "I" character of God as he is in himself. "To know, to will, and to act like God as the One who loves in himself and in his relationship means (in confirmation of his I-ness) to be a person. God is a person in this way, and he alone is a person in this way."[45] The being of God in act points to a life and personalness that belongs to the inner being of God prior to God's acting, living, and personal relation for us.

c. *God as one who loves*

This active, living, personal way of God's being within the Trinity leads us to the other attribute that belongs to God as God, to God as he is in himself, namely, that "God is love." Again, we refer to the first disclosure of the name *Yahweh* to Moses. Patrick Miller has suggested that this term may properly be translated: "I will be who I will be *with you*."[46] Upon this reading, the primary disclosure of God's name and inner nature implies that God is God as one who is with us, who acts "for us" — who, therefore, acts in love. If God were not love in himself, we would not know how to interpret the great hymn to God's love in I John 4:7–21 with its repeated insistence upon the priority of God's way of loving over ours ("not that *we* loved . . . but that God loved . . ."). If God as God, apart from and without reference to anything or anyone else, were not love, but were so only as he is *pro nobis*, we would inevitably confuse *our* way of loving with God's way of loving.

God's love does not fit the human ideal of love. Luther spoke of the harsher elements of God's will and judgment as his "strange work of love."[47] God's love is "strange," because it corresponds to no model of love that we would recommend or adopt. God's love is unique and has nothing to do with our way of love, except to call it into radical question and judgment. God loves without respect to the quality or condition of the object of his love. God seeks the lost sheep of the house of Israel (Matt. 15:24; Luke 19:10); God does not call the righteous (Luke 5:31), but "while we were yet sinners Christ died for us" (Rom. 5:8). God's love shows its radical "otherness" by the fact that it constitutes an end in itself. It does not need to achieve any particular purpose or effect to be complete.[48] If God's love needed "another" object, if that object were not already existent in the divine life but in some way dependent upon the natural order — if any of that were true — we could have no hope, because then God's love would be just as contingent, just as weak and ineffective as human love. The love of God is complete and beneficial in itself; it does not need us. If it needed us, it could not help us.

The independent and self-sufficient nature of God's love is lost in much contemporary theology. On the basis of the claim that "what matters most to us is the way to model our relationship with God," Sallie McFague proposes the metaphor "friend" as a more adequate term for God than "Lord."[49] From the standpoint of our discussion so far, the problem with this conception is that it purposely places God on the level of human mutuality and mutual need. Furthermore, to suppose, as McFague does, that "our 'salvation' depends in part on ourselves, on our willingness and ability to work cooperatively,"[50] is to embrace what has always been considered a fundamental error in Protestant faith. McFague's view assumes that a theology of divine sovereignty leads to Christian quietism (a charge already leveled at Calvin by Jacob Arminius), it signals a fatal turn from the ultimate source of human liberation, and it invests our confidence and hope in the historical wreckage of human virtue. The love of God is effective precisely because it is self-derived and self-sufficient. God's love does, of course, need an object, but the object of God's love, the relationality without which we cannot think of love, is found within the divine life itself as God the Father loves the Son and Holy Spirit.

Because God's love differs so radically from human love, it cannot be restricted to the accomplishment of purposes deemed satisfactory to modern culture, as for instance, the realization of a bourgeois ideal of justice and community. To identify such an ideal with God's purposes, is to fail to recognize the application of God's love precisely where life is so very *unlovable* — among the poor, diseased, resentful (and possibly drugged and violent) oppressed who wait for liberation. Unlike human love, God's love does not conflict with justice, but includes it. That is why God's love is liberating, why it "strangely" judges what is unloving and destroys what oppresses. Frederick Herzog writes of the social irony displayed on a southern billboard that warned: "Escape God's justice — flee to his love."[51] Those who claim exemption from the struggle of liberation need to be reminded that they cannot escape from God's justice to God's love, because in God justice and love are the same.

The human ideal of love may inspire and uplift; it may lead to greater acts of charity and more responsible living, but it cannot provide what is needed to bring about fundamental change in the human heart and human society. That can only be done by a transcendent love, a love expressive of the life and action of God, of a fact and reality which stands before and above all other reality. The cause of human liberation — liberation from despair, disease, poverty, oppression, and injustice — is not well served by the shifting commitments and contingencies of our kind of loving, or even by a divine love modeled after it. The accomplishment of liberation depends upon the love of God, the love of God *as* God. True liberation requires a sense of the absolute freedom of the God who acts in love.

2

The Structure of Divine Freedom

Introduction

If the evening news is any guide, the United States has in more ways than one "divested" itself of South African "interest." It no longer engages the public's attention that violence continues.[1] Having to some extent succeeded in economic disinvestment, social action groups want to move on to other, less intractable, issues — such as the civil wars in Central America, the reunification of Germany, or the democratization of Eastern Europe. But perhaps the main reason for our avoidance of the struggle in South Africa is that we can see no way around the deadly logic of a conflict in which each side believes it is fighting for its life. In that situation both blacks and whites view justice and peace as mutually contradictory and self-defeating, but in Mamelodi, the great black township on the outskirts of Pretoria, something else has been going on. There Ellen and Nico Smith undertook to serve a God identified neither with white self-interest nor with black revolutionary rhetoric. In taking the highly improbable and risky step of moving into Mamelodi to serve a parish, of becoming the only white residents of a city of a half-million blacks in the grip of revolutionary fervor, the Smiths have borne witness to the possibilities of God when no human possibilities are at hand.[2]

For the sake of these possibilities for human liberation we must recover a sense of the unlimited freedom of God, because only in the transcendent being and power of God can the struggle for liberation discover new and redemptive resources and thereby be delivered from a self-projection that merely reduplicates oppression. In chapter 1 we noted that a sense of the "otherness" of God cannot be achieved by abstraction or by avoiding anthropomorphisms. We argued that to reach the deity of God we have to begin with the humanity of God, with the revelation of God's freedom *for* us in Christ. Yet, because God reveals himself in Christ as really "God," we were led necessarily from God's freedom for us to a consideration of the way that God is free in himself, to the way that God is *as* God. In asserting the necessity of this movement from the outer to the inner nature of God, from the way God is for us to the way that God is in himself, we are not suggesting anything strange or new. The logic involved appeared inescapable even to Kant. "It concerns us not so much to know what God is in himself (his nature) as what he is for us . . . [but] to know the latter we must conceive and comprehend all the attributes of the divine nature . . . which, in their totality, are requisite to the carrying out of the divine will in this regard."[3]

In our first probing of this divine nature we learned that God is one who acts, lives, and loves in freedom. When we say that God lives and loves in himself prior to his action in love toward the whole creation, and when we have noted that God's living and love take place in radical freedom, then we have said the essential thing that must be said concerning the way God is as God. All other so-called attributes are finally subsumable under the notation that God acts in love. Here, however, we are particularly interested in how the radical freedom of God forms the basis and hope of human liberation, and so we must look more closely at the way God is free in himself and the way this freedom determines God's action in love. From this perspective the freedom of God appears to disclose itself in four ways: (1) that God is free *in* himself; (2) that God is free *from* any other power, thing, or person; (3) that God is free *for* the other things and persons he has made; and finally, (4) that God is free *from* his freedom *for* us.[4] In what follows we will analyze these four aspects of divine freedom and show how each informs and empowers the struggle for liberation.

I. God's Freedom in Himself

God's freedom *in* himself means that God's action and love do not require any other being outside of himself for their actualization and realization. In himself God is free. This radical and

ineffable freedom of God finds clearest expression in the term
aseity, which comes from the compound *a se*, meaning "from the
self" or "self-derived." Aseity obviously cannot be applied to
created being, which can be and act only in a causal nexus and
thus *ab alio*, "from another."[5]

To say that God is free in himself means that God does not need
any other being, because in a sense, God already possesses all
things. As Barth has noted, if

> we say that God is *a se* . . . we say that he is the one who
> already has and is in himself everything that would have to be
> the object [or purpose] of his creation and causation if he were
> not he, God.[6]

Note carefully that this statement does not equate God with
everything that is, as if God's work of creation did not bring to
pass something new and other than himself. God "already has
and is in himself" *not* everything that God creates, but rather,
God has in himself every possible attribute and characteristic that
could be assigned as a reason or purpose of his creation. Just as
God's love does not need an object apart from and outside of the
divine selfhood to be actual and real, so too the power, wisdom,
and majesty of God do not require anything apart from God to be
real. God is not creative because he brought the universe into
being, but the universe came into being because God was already
creative. God possesses the attribute of "power" not because he
rules creation; rather, God governs the creation because he is
already and antecedently powerful.

This point calls for emphasis, because if God's love, power,
and justice were not first of all his own, then it would be difficult
to imagine how God's freedom could liberate human beings from
the oppressive ambiguities of finite love, power, and justice. As
Reinhold Niebuhr and Paul Tillich have shown, hatred, oppression and injustice are the result of the inherent incapacity of their
opposites to find unambiguous actualization under the conditions of existence.[7] If the love, power, and justice of God were like
ours and not antecedently his, then we would have no reason to
hope for a way out of the conflicting demands of *our* justice —
respecting, for instance, the conflict between individual and
community rights in judicial and penal systems, or the conflict
between the right to privacy and the public's need to know

respecting freedom of the press, AIDS testing, and a host of other issues. If God does not in the absolute aseity of his freedom possess power in a way quite different from the operation of power in the world, we would have no basis for the hope that the power of God may yet liberate us from the danger that accompanies every exercise of "our" power, including its final threat — nuclear annihilation.

II. God's Freedom from Other Being

Only on the basis of this prior freedom that God has *in* himself can we now go on to say that God is also free *from* other being. This second form of God's freedom flows from the first,

> If [God] does not need his own being or any basis or limitation in himself, if he has and is in himself being, ground and limit in the actuality of his existence and in the freedom proper to him, how can he possibly need any other being, or need to be grounded or limited by it?[8]

This means that the God of the Bible, the one who in absolute freedom "laid the foundation of the earth" (Job 38:4), cannot be associated with Whitehead's God, whose "primordial" or creative nature is balanced by a "consequent" or contingent nature fully dependent upon the "actual entities" of the world in the process of their becoming.[9] Even less can such a God be confused with Hartshorne's cruder formulation of God as "maximal being," who is still but "one power among others."[10] Nor can we identify a God who is free from other being with Kaufman's God, who is merely "the complex of physical, biological, and historico-cultural conditions which have made human existence possible."[11] If God is free and needs no other being, then the existence of other being cannot stand over against God as that upon which God's existence must somehow be contingent. To the contrary, if God is free in himself, the existence of the cosmos must be a product of, and thus subordinate to, his will.

The freedom of God *from* other being is expressed primarily in the well-known doctrine of creation out of nothing (*creatio ex nihilo*). "In the beginning God . . . " With these opening words of Genesis the Bible sets the proper course for theological reflection. We must begin with God, before whom and beside whom there is in the beginning no other. The fact that in Gen. 1:2 the priestly poet envisions God brooding over (apparently) preexistent "waters" in his work of creation does not contradict the claim that God created out of nothing.[12] Neither is the doctrine embarrassed by the absence of specific reference to a creation out of nothing in Genesis 1 and 2. In these poems God must be seen to create out of nothing, because in the work of creation there is nothing beside God which would have to be understood (as it is in other creation myths) as an eternal substance which intrudes into the creation as a non-divine or negative principle, setting itself over against God and constituting for God a limit.[13] Moreover, we must say that God creates *ex nihilo*, because in Genesis 1 God creates simply by his word. "And God said . . . and it was so" (Gen. 1:9, 11, 14, 15, 24). In that litany of God's saying/doing, the poet obviously sees God pulling things, so to speak, "out of thin air."

If God creates out of nothing, then God obviously does not create out of himself. That much is also clear from the biblical witness. From the point of view of Genesis there can be no question of a Neoplatonic overflowing of ultimate being into the emptiness of non-being.[14] God exists as other than that which he creates, and creation exists as other than God. This point, too, is important for our study, because if God holds himself distinct and free from his creation, then the creation has its own reality, integrity, and responsibility. Human being is addressed by God as to an other.[15] And if this human being cannot escape its dependency upon God, it nevertheless has its own finite reality and so, too, its own world and sphere of activity. The struggle for liberation takes place within this sphere. While in this book we are primarily interested in showing the *dependence* of human liberation upon the absolute freedom of God, human responsibility in its own time and place must always be assumed. We are not left to ourselves, but we are nonetheless responsible for what we can do.

We must also note that even though it is other than God, the creation does not *per se* restrict the freedom of God. The world does not constitute a "problem" for God. The christological controversies of the fourth and fifth centuries were in large measure a result of the mistaken conviction that, because from our side *finitum non capax infinitum* (the finite is not capable of the infinite), the same disability must to some extent operate on God's side. The chasm separating the human and the divine appeared to theologians like Nestorius and Apollinarius to be as unbridgeable from God's side as from ours. Theological understanding of the incarnation was rendered all the more difficult, because the distance separating divine and human reality seemed to them to constitute an order which could not be set aside without contradicting God's own nature.

The God who is free in himself, however, is also free from other being. God enters into the creation in the most intimate of ways, but he does not bind himself to it. God does not become part of the nexus of cause and effect that governs all reality other than himself. *Deus non est in genere*. This dictum of the Scholastics needs to be taken with greater seriousness than they themselves took it. God did not, even in the act of incarnation, become a part of the creature's genus or class. On this basis we have been able to say that the freedom of God provides a love, power, and justice radically and redemptively different from our own.

The freedom of God *from* other being gives hope to the struggle for liberation, for what prospect could faith have for the attainment of real justice if God were subject to its ineluctable contradictions? Liberation requires a justice strong enough to overcome the contradictions and failures of human justice. Today, after two centuries of revolutionary effort, social, economic, and political oppression continue around the globe. Even where oppression has been overcome, as in the case of the current liberation of Eastern Europe from communism, the resurgence of ancient rivalries, racial prejudice, and religious violence raise the question as to whether authentic freedom has been achieved. The universal tendency to deny real freedom in favour of a bondage to self-interest will defeat every theology of liberation unless it has before it a God who is free *from* his creation so that he can be free *for* it by breaking into and through the inevitabilities that control human existence.

III. God's Freedom for Us

Everything that has been said so far about the freedom of God *in* himself and *from* other being holds theological relevance only because it contributes to an understanding of the fact that God is free *for* us. When we first began to consider the freedom of God we admitted that Christian thought really begins at this point — with the way that God makes himself free for us (*pro nobis*) in Jesus Christ; but because the God who is in Christ is *God*, we had to move from God as he is for us to God as he is in himself. Thus we addressed the specific question of the nature of divine freedom — the internal freedom of God and the freedom of God from the creation. Armed with these findings, we now come full circle and are in a position to consider more carefully the point with which we began — the freedom of God *for* us.

The freedom of God for us represents the sum of the gospel and includes all the liberating activity of Jesus — his teaching, his mighty acts of healing, his deliverance of captives from sin and death through his own death and resurrection. For this reason theologies of liberation are surely right in promoting a "Christology from below" which permits us to discern the freedom of God for us in the life of Jesus and his call to discipleship.[16] We shall have more to say about the liberating activity of Jesus in subsequent chapters. Here we are concerned with the *primary* form of God's freedom for us as expressed in the prologue to the Gospel of John: "And the Word became flesh and dwelt among us, full of grace and truth" (vs. 14). The freedom of God for us presents itself first of all in the freedom of God to be radically and totally *with* us.

This claim may appear at first to be an accommodation to the theologies of divine immanence as represented, for example, by Georg W. F. Hegel and Alfred North Whitehead. But there is a difference. Immanentist theologies do not understand the presence of God to be a function of his unique freedom. Because they do not see God in the light of the freedom God has in himself and from all other being, God in these systems identified with some other, perhaps higher, reality such as history (Hegel) or life (Bergson) or entities (Whitehead). These views undermine a sense of the reality of God, because when God becomes "one power among others" (Hartshorne) or one entity among others (Whitehead) — when, in other words, we abandon the absolute freedom which belongs to God, the question arises as to whether it is really "God" who is understood to be present in the creation. On the other hand, when (as in Hegel and more recently in

Kaufman) we so identify God with humanity that the attributes which belong to the divine nature are transferred to creaturely being, the question arises as to whether we have anymore a real human creatureliness with which God can be present. The much desired solidarity of God and creation collapses in immanentist theologies since the presence both of God and human being are removed by redefinition.

A God who is unequivocally free and therefore also free from other being and the limiting causal relations which belong to it — such a God (and only such a God) is free to be for other being by being with it in unrestricted immanence. The freedom of God to be for and with his creation does not cancel his freedom from it; otherwise "the light that shines in the darkness" (John 1:5) would be overcome by darkness. Even in the completeness of the incarnation, the God who died on a cross and rose on the third day does not become part of finite being so as to become wholly subject to its conditions. When we said above that God, even in the most intimate connection with creation, does not "become part of the nexus of cause and effect," and when we will claim below that God is free to enter the human condition without abandoning his supreme and transcendent lordship, we are merely making a point always considered essential to the doctrine of incarnation. Calvin insisted that, while God is revealed and is at work in Christ, there is also a being and work of God *ad extra*—apart from the incarnation.

"Without leaving heaven he willed to be born in the virgin's womb, to go about the earth, and to hang on a cross; yet he continually filled the world even as he had from the beginning."[17] This doctrine, sometimes called the *extra Calvinisticum*, runs the risk of diverting attention from the nature and will of God revealed in Christ to some other character and work of God *ad extra* — a risk clearly displayed in Calvin's conception of the "hidden" and "terrible" decree of God in his doctrine of election. This danger notwithstanding, the freedom of God must be maintained even in the incarnation, otherwise the *kenosis* or "emptying" of the Son into humanity as described in Eph. 2:7 would not be so much a sacrifice as a suicide of divinity, indeed, a "death of God."

That God is radically with his creation does not mean that created being loses its own identity and proper freedom. Again, we find useful instruction in the Yahwist narrative in

Genesis, chapters 2 and 3. God is present in the Garden. No difference or distinction impedes God's address to the man and the woman or their hearing of God's word. How could it be otherwise since God created them both — "by hand," one might say. God remains with the woman and the man and provides what they need. Moreover, God's intimate presence and support does not violate God's freedom or the freedom given to the man and woman. They still possess their own individual identities and responsibilities. They can decide against God, and they do so. However, against Hegel and, more recently, Tillich, we must insist that the fact that they do so does not establish their freedom, but merely exposes their attempt to forfeit it. God's immanence was not a threat to their individuality before their decision and "fall," nor was God's presence afterward a threat to their freedom. To the contrary, only because God sought and found them, clothed them, and provided for their future could they face that future freely. God accompanied them out of paradise.

The remarkable immanence of God was made manifest in Jesus Christ. Unless we can see God's way of being for us here, it is doubtful that it can be seen at all. This is why the doctrine of the incarnation is so essential for the cause of human liberation. The liberating freedom of God must be seen in the complete unity of his divinity with the humanity of Jesus; otherwise we would have no basis upon which to hope for its redemptive presence in our political, racial, and sexual existence. As Gregory of Nazianzus said, "That which is unassumed is unhealed," and, we might add, "unliberated."[18] If God is with us in radical solidarity in a way impossible for any thing or person to be with and for another, then a theology of liberation has available to it a hope, confidence, and power not to be found in any other revolutionary theory or movement. The failure of Marxism to achieve its revolutionary goals should stand as a warning to those liberation movements, whether racial, sexual, or political, which isolate their own experience of oppression from the presence of God incarnate. That it is *God* and not some self-projected apotheosis of human need, but God in absolute freedom, who wills to be with us in the struggle for liberation, means that the human future is not trapped in the self-perpetuating circle of injustice which has marked the struggle for liberation throughout human history.

Furthermore, the immanence of God in human affairs means that, in contradistinction from all other sources of revolutionary change, God does not need to destroy human being or subvert the structures of existence which delimit its identity and integrity. As God's way of being radically present does not threaten the being of the one with whom he unites himself, so God requires no Hegelian *Aufhebung* (either as "lifting up" or "dissolution") of human history and culture into some angelic state in order to save it. Peter Hodgson asserts that the dynamic of freedom in history (which "in its most concrete form is God") operates according to a "dialectic of determinate negation [which] means that the reality of history is inescapably conflictual."[19] While conflict and negation in history is a fact and *appears* inevitable, the cause of this condition may be understood better as human resistance to, than as an expression of, the divine will. The freedom of God ought never to be identified with what we view as historically "inescapable."

A theology of liberation has no need or reason to accept the assumption, common to revolutionary idealism of every sort, that all inherited structures of human community are unredeemable and must be replaced by what is claimed to be, but cannot be, something new. Of course, within the structures of human history there are what Tillich has called "structures of destruction" which are not of, but against, human community.[20] Forms of male oppression, of child abuse and neglect, of economic exploitation, of political oppression and military violence — all these and more constitute negative structures with which God does not identify and from which God would liberate us. To discriminate correctly between destructive and constructive forms of human life is always risky and necessarily a matter of prayer and guidance. Nevertheless, it would surely be wrong to imagine that all inherited forms of life are dispensable, or that a God who wills to be immanent in human affairs cannot exercise the liberating power of his grace in and through the structures of family, church, the state, and commerce.

We have, therefore, no cause to imagine that the presence of God which sustains individuality and personal integrity cannot work through sexual, racial, and other inherent forms of human selfhood. If God wills to be immanent in creation, his liberating power and presence may be found in all the rich variety of our ways of being human together. If God's revolution works to overthrow structures of destruction, it can also work within other structures of existence to transform and redirect human intentions and expectations for the pursuit of justice. If the freedom of God can create new structures of life for women, it can also work through the nuclear family. If it can work through the American form of government, it can also work through other political forms — single party systems in the new nations of Africa or a socialist democracy in Nicaragua. If it can work through racial self-consciousness among those whose identity has been insulted by claims of white supremacy, it can also achieve liberation through interracial and non-racial visions of community; if through communism, also through agrarian and capital intensive forms of commerce; if through violent revolutions, such as the American and French, then also through pacifist protests of violence. These and scores of other possibilities for the operation of God's freedom in human affairs mean that the theologies of liberation may engage in the struggle for freedom and justice without rejecting the immeasurable variety of our ways of being human and God's ways of being with us.

IV. God's Freedom from His Freedom For

An analysis of the meaning of the freedom of God in its various forms for human liberation comes now to the last and fourth form of that freedom — a form which can only be described in a reflexive and dialectical way. We have said that God is free *in* himself and free *from* the creation in order to be really and radically free *for* it — by being *with* it in Jesus Christ. Now just as God's act of creation did not bind God to creaturely being so as to curtail or limit his freedom, so too God's freedom for us by being immanently with us does not change the fact that God is free — free even in respect to his solidarity with us. As in all other of God's attributes, God's immanence is not determined by our ways of being present. Just as divine grace does not preclude judgment, so God's way of being present does not preclude his concealment and withdrawal. For this reason we must understand the final form of divine freedom as God's freedom *from* his freedom *for* — or, more precisely, God's freedom from any *particular* manifestation of his freedom for us.

This clarification is important, because if from our perspective the ways of God must appear contradictory, from the divine point of view they are not. God's actions are indeed necessary and determined, but determined only by the free exercise of his sovereign will. Again, we will follow Barth's analysis.

> In this his freedom, in which he spontaneously binds himself in a certain way to the world, [God] remains unbound from the point of view of the world and its determinations. His changelessness does not correspond with any one of our constancies. His faithfulness is his own, and not the metaphysical equivalent of any one of the normal features of creaturely existence.[21]

So God may reveal himself in immanence ("The heavens declare the glory of God," Psalm 19) or conceal himself in withdrawal ("Truly thou art a God who hidest thyself," Isa. 45:14). In responding to prayer or withholding judgment, God is free to be conditioned or unconditioned in his relation to the world. As creator of the natural order God can obviously work within it according to its laws or, if we care to accept the testimony of scripture, God is free to operate upon nature from the infinite distance of divinity in the form of miracle. God is free to relate to people in the most intimate way ("As one whom his mother comforts, so I will comfort you," Isa. 66:13) or to confront them in thunder and lightning on Mt. Sinai. God is free to become human in Jesus Christ and to assume again the distance of the Godhead. In the same way, God is free to enter the human condition as the lowliest and humblest of servants without abandoning his supreme and transcendent lordship.[22]

God in freedom can be and do all this and more, for in scripture there is no single way of God's being for us that does not have its dialectical counterpart and opposite. This means that, when we consider all the ways in which the freedom of God empowers and sustains the struggle for human liberation, we are confronted with surprising possibilities. The variety of God's ways of being free for us arises not only from his immanence in the world, but also from the infinite capacity of God to act in love toward creation in ways which must appear opposite and contradictory to any of those other ways. If, for example, according to his immanence, God may work through a variety of political forms, he may work as well through none at all. The protest of nihilism (which must appear to us dangerous) or charismatic enthusiasm (which must appear to us irrelevant) may also be vehicles of God's liberating action.[23] If God's presence in history seems usually to involve social and political struggle, who can say whether, as in the Middle Ages and as Thomas Merton in our time has suggested, the life of contemplation might not be an equally effective instrument of God's justice?[24] If God is always on the side of the poor, his way of being so cannot be determined or defined by the conditions of poverty or by the expectations of the impoverished. If the freedom of God inspires a liberating self-acceptance and even self-celebration among women whose self-consciousness has been victimized by centuries of oppression, it may also (and contradictorily) promote their emancipation through a self-denial that comes from the security of faith. Finally, and perhaps most unexpectedly of all, if in the pursuit of justice, socialism has seemed "always . . . most helpful in its specific time and place,"[25] it seems now to be the case (at least in Eastern Europe and the Soviet Union) that the mechanics of capitalism in the free and miraculous providence of God may also be employed in the service of human liberation.

To summarize: The freedom of God *in* himself promises a love, power, and justice redemptively different from our own. The freedom of God *from* other being assures us that God's liberating activity can overcome the nexus of cause and effect that renders human revolutions ambiguous and ineffective. The freedom of God *for* us means that God joins with us so radically that no form of oppression is alien to his concern, nor any human instrument unusable in his work of liberation. Finally, the freedom of God *from* his ways of being *for* us means that God's liberating activity will often appear to us surprising, even contradictory, so that even the most unlikely and unpromising elements of human life and culture may be employed in God's revolution.

These dialectical possibilities do not mean that what, on the basis of scripture and disciplined reflection, seems necessary for workable political change ought to be set aside in favor of other and less promising approaches. These dialectical possibilities do suggest, however, that in responding to God's liberating power through an active participation in the struggle for liberation (by advocacy of the poor, by combating racism and sexism and violence), we can never forget that we are dealing with a God who is radically and absolutely free. If we deny God any of the possibilities mentioned above — or others we do not see — we are, as Barth reminds us: "denying God himself. Instead of recognizing and adoring God, we are setting up an idol. For we are imposing upon him — in defiance of the freedom which he has actually proved to us — a bondage which can only be that of our own self will that would like to deny God and put itself in the place of God."[26]

In conclusion, we need to raise a question and offer a further point of clarification. The question is this: In speaking of God's freedom *from* other being, God's freedom *for* creation by being immanent *within* it, and especially in speaking of God's unpredictable freedom *from* his way of being free *for* us, have we raised so many possibilities in respect to God's will and work in the world that we will lose our way entirely? Are we construing the freedom of God in such a way that we can know nothing of God with certainty, and thus have no assurance of what obedience to God's call for liberation means or how it should be pursued? In subsequent chapters (especially chapters 5 and 6) we will attempt to give further assurance on this point. Now we can say that, just as God's own inner purposes are neither capricious nor contradictory, so too we have not been left with unprincipled unpredictability.

In the first place, when we said that God is free to enter into human life and also free to return to the sphere of divine transcendence, we were simply describing how the freedom of God expressed itself in Jesus Christ. In Christ we see definitively what it means that God limits himself without forfeiting his unlimitedness, how God reveals himself and conceals himself, how God judges and saves. But the question may remain as to whether the prior freedom of God may not impose upon God's action in Christ an uncertainty and caprice which overrides that meaning of his freedom. If Arius had been right, if the Son of God in the flesh were not also the Son, the eternal Logos; if the one we see in Jesus Christ were not also "in the beginning with God," then this danger would be real. But in light of the identity of Jesus Christ and the revelation of the inner life of God found in him, we have to recognize the freedom of God in all its forms as an activity controlled by love, which must become the first principle of every revolutionary effort. Furthermore, because the inner and prior freedom of God cannot be viewed apart from its disclosure in Jesus Christ, we have no reason to interpret God's freedom (even that hidden in the mystery of trinitarian existence) as having any meaning or purpose other than that of grace and good for his creation. That is why the radical and absolute freedom of God in any of its forms can mean for us nothing else than liberation from everything that threatens and oppresses human existence.

The freedom of God means liberation from many things — certainly liberation from sin and guilt and death, and certainly also liberation for "the glorious freedom that belongs to the children of God" (Rom. 8:21). In our time and situation it also means, and in many contexts must mean primarily, liberation from economic and political oppression. Human liberation is God's cause before it is ours; God took up this work before we did and will finish it when our best efforts come to an end. If we wish to rally to this cause and participate in God's revolution, we can never forget that it is with *God* that we have to do — not a God who is subject to the oppressive and hopeless conditions of finitude, and certainly not a God we can define, limit, or control, but a God who is utterly and radically free and therefore free for us. To the extent that we remember this essential fact in our pursuit of justice, we must always ask whether our judgments concerning the will and activity of God originate in our own self-understanding or in God's self-revelation — whether our programs and strategies for human liberation are responsive to the revealed will of God or are merely projections of our own assumptions and values.

Obedience to the will of a God who is mysteriously, absolutely, and radically free will always mean that we must live and work by faith and not by sight. But however uncertain, unpredictable, and marvelously varied the specific ways of God's freedom (and thus our obedience to it) may be, we are not left without a guide along the way. The counsel that Calvin gives is still correct — that we should look to Christ "the mirror wherein we must, and without self-deception may, contemplate" the ways and works of God.[27] Thus our responsibilities in respect to the liberating will and activity of God are the same as those announced by Jesus in Nazareth when he claimed for himself the prophecy of Isaiah,

The spirit of the Lord is upon me,
because he has anointed me to preach
   good news to the poor.
He has sent me to proclaim release to
   the captives
and recovering of sight to the blind,
   to set at liberty those who are oppressed,
to proclaim the acceptable year of the Lord.

Luke 4:18–19

3

Thinking about God

Introduction

If the Christian church is to serve the cause of human liberation in the name of him who "set at liberty those who are oppressed," it must keep before it the freedom of God. It must in its thought and action avoid projecting upon the image of God its own values and preoccupations, for only a God who is really "God" can accomplish liberation. In the previous chapter we considered how the fourfold freedom of God empowers the struggle for freedom. Now we have to face a question we have so far avoided. If we cannot deny Barth's assertion that we inevitably think of God by projecting our own image, that "we all in any case are idolaters," then the question arises: Is it really possible to think authentically about God as he is in himself, and if so, what kind of thinking is that?

To begin to answer this question, we must first undertake a short excursion into the history of Western metaphysics. By "thinking" we do not mean just any form of mental activity, such as emotion, intuition, or a mere contentless consciousness of reality. We mean here by "thinking" what Robert Scharlemann has described as the activity of mind by which we bring to consciousness "something as what that thing is in itself."[1] I may "experience" a tree by its falling on me and not have time to think of it as a tree. A painting of trees may evoke an emotion from me which has nothing to do with trees themselves. I may be vaguely conscious of a tree outside my study window without thinking of it. But if I "think" of a tree, I must in some sense reflect upon its nature — what it is in itself — and that means I must distinguish my own thinking about the tree from the tree itself. Similarly, if I wish to think of abstract qualities such as "justice" or "beauty" as real, then I must think of them as other than my own thinking about them. So too, of course, with thinking about God.

How it happens that I can thus "think" about a material or spiritual object as real in itself (as other than my thinking about it) has constituted the fundamental problem of Western philosophy. Classical realism, as represented by Plato and Aristotle, explained the relation between thought and reality by proposing that the "reality" of a thing like a tree or a concept like beauty resides in a transcendent and unchangeable "form" or "idea." The "form" of "treeness" or "beauty itself" finds reflection both in the object (the tree or beautiful thing, according to Aristotle) *and* in thought, but belongs to neither. Thus when I think of a tree, I am thinking of a reality other than my own thinking — but also (and this is the problem of Platonism) of a reality not exactly identical with the biological object either. According to this philosophy, thinking about God is essentially no different from thinking about any other transcendent reality. The problem, of course, is that, if God can be thought in the same way as "treeness," "beauty," or "justice," it is difficult to think of God as really other than such concepts.

In the fourteenth and fifteenth centuries nominalism sought to protect the integrity of objects, whether material or mental, by asserting that the reality of "treeness" or "beauty" was not dependent upon some transcendent form, but was simply the name (*nomos*) that we assign to similar experiences. For nominalists like William of Occam, thought about God, because it is not derived from worldly phenomena, was distinguished from other kinds of thought and made dependent upon revelation. Nominalism laid the groundwork for modern science, because the knowledge of ordinary reality was no longer sought in a transcendent spiritual realm, but in the world of experience. According to this view, truth about God comes by way of supernatural enlightenment, but we arrive at the truth about objects by thinking of them in their relation to other objects.

This assumption about the knowledge of objects was challenged by David Hume in the eighteenth century. Hume noted that the sensations which supply the raw material for our thinking of a tree are different for each person, and thus each "thinks" a different tree. Now if objects cannot be distinguished from each person's thought about them, they lose their "objective" character, they lose their reality. This reasoning led Hume to question the reality of objects external to the mind. He did not, however, fall into the solipsism of George Berkeley, because his theory of imagination and memory, which employed the principles of coherence and continuity, allowed the reality of objects *not* immediately perceived to be asserted. One does not see a door, but hears a familiar sound and a person approaching in the room.

> The present phenomenon is a contradiction to all past experience, unless the door, which I remember on t'other side the chamber, be still in being . . . I have . . . to suppose the continued existence of objects in order to connect their past and present appearances . . . [thus] I am naturally led to regard the world, as something real and durable, and as preserving its existence, even when it is no longer present to my perception.[2]

Although Hume recovered a sense of the reality of things apart from our experience of them, he continued to doubt the knowability of metaphysical ideas like "order," "causation," and, of course, "God."

The problem is that we cannot think without employing metaphysical ideas. If the idea "God" is not necessary for thought, "order," "goodness," and the like are. Thus it remained for Immanuel Kant to move philosophy beyond Hume's epistemological roadblock by arguing that, while we cannot know the "thing itself" (*Ding an sich*), we can know the truth about it. If the mind cannot know an object independently of the thinker's sensory experience, it nevertheless possesses objective knowledge. This Kant could assert because, for him, "knowledge" was not simply the result of the impact of things upon the senses, but was the result of the activity of the mind. In his *Critique of Pure Reason*, Kant argued that the mind shapes experience by way of certain "categories" (time, space, quality, etc.) which, while belonging to the mind, have a universal and thus an objective status. I cannot get on the other side of my senses and know the tree "in itself," but I can think of the tree as it is apart from my thinking if the *way* I think of it conforms to universal categories of time, space, causality, etc. I can also know the abstract qualities of things (goodness, beauty, etc.) on the same basis. Kant was careful to note, however, that such knowledge applies only to the world of finite experience. It cannot be applied to an infinite being, to God, who for Kant could not be an object of knowledge, but only a "postulate of practical reason."

How then are we to think of God? After the demise of classical realism and nominalism, and in spite of the radical skepticism of Hume, we have, with the help of Kant, found ways of thinking about both physical and mental objects as real. But how are we to think of God who is not an object like other objects to which a knowing subject can assign independent reality? If "thinking" deals with things finite and contingent, how are we to "think" authentically about God who is infinite and absolute — who is radically free from and other than all the conditions and categories in terms of which we think? If the cause of human liberation requires a faith in (and thus thinking about) the freedom of God, this question cannot be avoided.

I. The Bible and Critical Thought

The Bible has its own way of answering this question. In the story of Job, for instance, Job's thinking about God, in spite of a good deal of prior and rather sophisticated theologizing by himself and his "friends," becomes authentic at the place where God asks, "Who is this that darkens counsel with words without knowledge?" And Job confesses, "I uttered what I did not understand" (Job 42:3). The fact that language about God must be self-critical appears in the book of Job to form the precondition of authentic theological reflection. This first step of critical thinking about God is then followed by a second criticism in which not only Job's thoughts, but Job himself is called into question by God's final declaration, "I will question you and you shall declare unto me" (42:4).

Scripture generally recognizes the incapacity of human thought to grasp God as its object. That God is nevertheless known in the Bible depends upon God's self-revelation. The apprehension of revelation, however, includes on the human side a double movement which involves first, a critical assessment of thought about God (as not thought about *God*, but as "darkened counsel . . . without knowledge"), and second, a critical awareness which places the *thinker* in a crisis, literally a "crossing," where thought is "doubled crossed" and reversed so that the one who must question the validity of his or her thought about God becomes the object of God's thought ("I will question you").

The claim that thought about God involves a movement in which criticism is applied first to thought and then to the thinker appears typical of the major theophanies of the Old Testament. Standing before the burning bush, Moses confesses that his thought and language about God are not adequate. "They will not believe me . . . I am slow of speech and tongue . . . send, I pray, some other person." This first self-criticism is then followed by a second (meta-)criticism in which Moses, the thinking subject, becomes the object of "the anger of the Lord . . . kindled against Moses." Most significantly, in this second criticism the object of Moses' thought becomes the subject thinking Moses' thought and speech. "I will be in your mouth . . . and teach you" (Exod. 4:10–16).

The movement just described from *apophatic* thought (denial of what is claimed by speech) to *theophanic* thought (God provides what is claimed) is typical also of other such confrontations in the Bible. Isaiah's notation that our thoughts are inadequate for thoughts about God (Isa. 55:8) finds early illustration in his famous call (Isa. 6:1–9). His verbal inability to express the reality of the Lord he sees "high and lifted up" is a problem not only of his thought, but of the fact that he himself is "a man of unclean lips." It is only after his lips were touched with the burning coal and his sins forgiven that God tells him how to speak: "Go, and say to this people." Given the "difference" which marks all language about God, we should not be surprised that Isaiah's message was "Hear and hear, but do not understand, see and see, but do not perceive." Similarly, Jeremiah's recognition of his intellectual incapacity ("Ah, Lord God, behold I do not know how to speak") had to advance to the place where he himself was the object of God's action ("the Lord put forth his hand and touched my mouth"), so that again God became the subject speaking through the prophet. "Behold, I have put my words in your mouth" (Jer. 1:6–9).

The same is true in the New Testament. Prior to his conversion, Paul's language about God could only be characterized as contradictory to the truth of God, for Paul was "breathing threats and murder" against the faith (Acts 9:1). Thus it was not just his theological understanding, but his whole being that was called into question on the road to Damascus. "He fell to the ground . . . and when his eyes were opened he could see nothing" (9:4, 8). Only in such extremity of loss and incapacity could he learn what it meant to be "a chosen instrument" of God and to have the "scales [fall] from his eyes" (9:15, 18).

This experience may well have been the source of Paul's reflection upon thought about God in his letter to the Galatians. Here he also sees a double movement. "Formerly," he wrote to the Galatians, "when you did not know God, you were in bondage to beings which by nature are no gods" (Gal. 4:8). "Formerly," that is, when they *thought* they knew God and were content to think quite uncritically about him, they did not know God. In spite of the intellectually rich religious milieu in which they lived, they, like their neighbors in Ephesus, were "strangers to the covenant of promise, having no hope and without God in the world" (Eph. 2:12). But the Galatians to whom Paul wrote had heard the gospel — a message of liberation from sin and death. The hearing and acceptance of this good news required of them repentance (*metanoia*), a turning away from sin and self-reliance. In respect to their thinking about God this meant not only a first critical movement exposing the incapacity of their thought and language about God, but also a second movement, a *metanoein*, a second or after-thinking in which they found themselves to be in crisis at the intersection where God's action and thought replaced their own. That is what lies behind Paul's remarkable concluding declaration to the Galatians, "But now . . . you have come to know God, *or rather to be known by God*" (Gal. 4:19).

In light of the biblical witness we may advance the following thesis: *Thinking about God is possible only upon the basis of God's own action, and it involves human thought in a metacritical movement. This movement calls into question not only thought about God, but also the thinker, who thereby is led into a new relationship in which thought and language about God becomes authentic.* In what follows, I want to analyze more carefully the nature of this metacritical movement. This will be done, first, by reference to Ludwig Feuerbach and the philosophy of deconstruction, which provide examples of the first critique; next by reviewing proposals of Robert Scharlemann regarding the second, metacritical element; and finally by examining Karl Barth's doctrine of the *analogia fidei*, which expresses the way God empowers human thought to think of God.

II. Toward Metacritical Thinking about God

A. *Feuerbach*

To the question of the possibility of thought about God as *God*, Ludwig Feuerbach gave an unequivocal and radically critical answer: "Man's knowledge of God is man's knowledge of himself, of his own nature . . . "[3] As we have seen, this critical insight was not unknown among the biblical writers. Nor was it lost on pagan antiquity. As one ancient skeptic put it, "If donkeys had gods they would bray."[4] What distinguishes Feuerbach's argument is the thoroughness of his critique of religious ideas.

In his *Essence of Christianity* Feuerbach argued that all religious conceptions are simply the result of human self-alienation and denial. What we ought to believe about ourselves, but do not because of oppressive authority or lack of understanding, we project upon the infinite and call "God." With this idea Feuerbach was able to show the anthropological origin of a vast number of biblical concepts. We assign creativity to God since "the happiest, the most blissful activity is that which is productive."[5] Atonement expresses our need for escape from guilt, resurrection the satisfied desire of personal existence after death, and miracle and sacraments our sense of the mystery and power in all finite things.

If we do not recognize the truth in Feuerbach's analysis, if we do not admit that our religious ideas are invariably expressions of human need and self-understanding, then we will not be able to make the first critical movement required for authentic thinking about God. Feuerbach is a useful guide through the first critique required for thinking about God, but he can take us no further, for he could not make the second, metacritical movement. He was unwilling to apply to the thinker the same critical judgment that he applied to thought about God, and thus his philosophy collapsed into a naive and romantic view of human nature and its divinity. Feuerbach believed that the qualities we project onto God really belong to human nature. As he put it, "the being of God is only thine own being which is an object to thee, and what presents itself *before* thy consciousness is simply what lies behind it."[6]

Feuerbach exhibits the result of the failure to submit to the critical presence of a God whose being is not human being and whose thoughts are precisely not human thoughts. Unless the second critical movement is made, then, however incisive a critique of religious ideas may be, it will inevitably reconstruct a "God" in terms more blatantly self-referential than before. Such a God, who represents "only thine own being" made "objective," may easily be co-opted to one's own cause, but will not serve the cause of human liberation. Indeed, we need to admit that a God who is nothing more or less than the aggrandizement of human presumption is the inspiration for every totalitarian government, every oppressive economy, and every human prejudice and injustice. If the cause of liberation imposes upon theology the need to recover the idea of a God who is free in himself as a guard against precisely those idolatries, we would do well to heed the lesson of Feuerbach. He could not sustain a radically critical perspective which throws the thinker into question. Here, perhaps, the philosophy of deconstruction offers a better (if also flawed) example.

B. *Deconstruction*

Discussions of deconstruction commonly begin with a disclaimer — and for good reason, because the movement takes as its central thesis that all attempts to discover an objective meaning in writing are doomed to failure and simply disclose the "logocentrism" by which Western thought has deluded itself since the rise of Greek philosophy. Thus deconstructionist texts appear immune from objective analysis. This problem notwithstanding, we may risk some observations.

Deconstruction was invented by Jacques Derrida, whose beginning point, according to John Searle, was a deep skepticism regarding the metaphysical foundations of knowledge.[7] As mentioned above, the Greeks found in such concepts as "truth," the "good," "the beautiful," etc., realities transcendent to the mind which account for the possibility of knowledge. After the nominalist critique of Platonic realism, the tendency, as seen in Kant, was to assign to such foundational concepts only a finite, but still universal, reality. Modern philosophy (e.g., logical positivism) has called into question the cogency and usefulness of such concepts. Derrida takes up the issue at this point, denies such ideas as "truth," "goodness," and "beauty" any reality at all, and becomes, in the words of J. Hillis Miller "a parricide . . . a bad son demolishing beyond hope of repair the machine of Western metaphysics."[8]

For Derrida, a deconstructionist analysis of "writing" reveals that, where we imagine that a text contains meaning, distinction, and objectivity, there is in fact nothing — only an "absence" in terms of which and in the presence of which we must find a way to exist. Using ideas developed by the Swiss linguist Ferdinand de Saussure, Derrida claims that language does not develop out of the experience of things, but out of an appreciation of distinction and "difference."[9] To employ a crude illustration, the meaning of the words "bed" and "sled," "cat" and "bat," depends upon the differences between their initial consonants rather than the objects to which they appear to refer. "Bed" = (not–*sl*ed). The presence of this "notness" is the presence of what Derrida calls "differ*a*nce."[10] It is this "differ*a*nce," this presence of what a text excludes, that constitutes for him the originating "trace" common to all language and thought.

> Differ*a*nce is what makes the movement of signification possible only if each element that is said to be "present" . . . is related to something other than itself but retains the mark of a past element and already lets itself be hollowed out by the mark of its relation to a future element. This trace relates no less to what is called the future than to what is called the past, and it constitutes what is called the present by this very relation to what it is not . . . In order for it to be, an interval must separate it from what it is not.[11]

Thus for Derrida "writing" must not be understood as inscription, but as the "trace" of absence, or void, that lies behind thought, speech, and written texts. On this basis Derrida can make the otherwise astonishing assertion that "there has never been anything but writing."[12]

In order to uncover the "trace" which lies at the base of thought and language, Derrida undertakes to "de-construct" a text to show how, in Robert Culler's words, "it undermines the philosophy it asserts."[13] "A deconstructive reading does not point out the flaws or weaknesses . . . of an author, but the *necessity* with which what he *does* see is systematically related to what he does *not* see."[14] In this method polar distinctions (good/bad, strong/weak, self/other) are discovered to be reversed in the text itself. Similarly, marginal and unimportant details will reveal the "tragic little secret" that language only refers to itself, or we might say, to what is excluded in it.[15]

Brahms once said of another composer: "His work may be immortal for quite some time." One is tempted to say the same of Derrida. His philosophy literally reeks with contradiction, because it denies ahead of time any correspondence between what language says and what it means. Again, as Searle has shown, if all language is self-referential and all texts self-contradictory, why do not deconstructionist texts *also* assert what they wish to deny, and in that way actually *re*construct metaphysics? In any case, as a philosophy deconstruction fails, because language works. If texts include contradiction, they also contain meaning — at least enough to build machines, erect political systems, and portray common emotional experiences.

In spite of its failure as philosophy, deconstruction from the perspective of theology may reflect a great and necessary truth. If language about the world does not function as deconstruction claims, language about God does. When applied to God, words can only remind us of "difference." This was the fundamental claim of Barth's first work, *The Epistle to the Romans*. There Barth speaks of the biblical text as a "crater," "void," "dry canal," and the like.[16] Language about God has for Barth a cuneiform quality. It has no content in and of itself, but merely points away from itself to what has already happened. "It is solely and exclusively *the something else* . . . which makes [the Bible] a witness."[17] As witness to the self-revelation of God, scripture can be understood only in terms of what it is not — "*not* right human thoughts . . . *not* the history of man . . . *not* the virtues of men . . . *not* [even] human standpoints."[18]

As we have mentioned earlier, "love," "power," "justice," etc., mean something *different* when they are applied to God, something in fact contradictory to what we ordinarily mean by those terms. Similarly, while we may have reason to believe that such metaphysical concepts as "causation," "time," and "space" correspond to realities of creaturely existence, we have no reason to think that they correspond in the same way to God's existence. God can make human beings free *for* time and space in revelation and incarnation, because he is in himself neither temporal nor spacial. Therefore, if the deconstruction of texts generally appears absurd, the deconstruction of religious texts, including the Bible, is logically necessary to make clear what the Bible already knows, namely, that in respect to our speaking of God we all have "unclean lips" (Isa. 6:5).

In contrast to Feuerbach, deconstruction approaches a metacritical perspective because it places the thinker at risk. But in the end it, too, is not critical enough. If it was thoroughly nihilistic, if it left the self standing before that terrible absence, it would better serve as a model of the metacritical movement we have in mind. But one cannot suppress the suspicion that in deconstruction the void created by the trace of difference and absence is surreptitiously filled by the spirit of humanity. At least it appears this way in the deconstructionist "a/theology" of Mark C. Taylor.

In spite of its undeniable stylistic brilliance, Taylor's *Erring* disappoints because it fails to capitalize on the theological possibilities of deconstruction. Instead, it lapses into a romantic indulgence of the self reminiscent of Nietzsche, who as Peter Hodgson has noted, is "the true genius behind the whole project."[19] The central theological idea of *Erring* involves the understanding of God as "writing."[20] This would be a startlingly innovative assertion if it were not for the fact that, as we have seen, "writing" in the deconstructionist lexicon does not mean inscription, but rather the ceaseless, eternal interplay of opposition and difference that produces language and thought. Thus the assertion that "God is writing" really reduces the idea of God to the inevitable self-referentiality of human thought. Taylor views his work as an extension of the "death of God" movement and so assumes that it is no longer possible to understand God as transcendent — certainly not for a "postmodern" culture in which not only religious claims but also claims of truth about human nature have been rendered meaningless.

According to deconstructionist analysis, human being is left in an eternal textuality of opposites, of the presence of absence — stranded without God, truth, or value. But, as both Searle and Hodgson have pointed out, the deconstructionists cannot themselves tolerate this situation. It is as impossible for Taylor as it was for Nietzsche. Taylor projects the "self" onto the hopeless hollowed-out landscape "of pure horizontality" where it can reign supreme.[21] Just as in Nietzsche the ego presides over the absolute truth of fate, so in Taylor the self finds ultimate and eternal significance as the "trace" of absence in "the never-ever-changing-same" of linguistic self-reference. For Taylor, the self takes on a divine status because it shares the function of divinity. Having been divested of transcendence, God is now merely "the divine milieu" — not a person or even a being, but merely a "place" occupied by our self-referentiality. The conclusion must be that, if God is "writing" and the self is "trace," God and the self are the same.

The cause of human liberation depends on a God who is really "God" and not a god who is "writing," who is only an absence occupied by the trace of human self-referentiality. Such a god can have no relevance for the cause of justice. As Peter Hodgson has put it,

> Taylor's God, it appears to me, is for those who don't need a real God . . . because they have all that life can offer . . . Taylor's God is a god for the children of privilege, not the children of poverty; a god for the oppressors, not the oppressed.[22]

If, to recover the freedom of God for human liberation, we need to learn to think of God as he is in himself and not as an extension of some aspect of our own self-understanding, then we will have to think more critically than the deconstructionist.

We have taken for our thesis that "thinking about God is possible only upon the basis of God's own action, and involves human thought in a metacritical movement. In this movement not only thought about God, but also thought about the thinker is called into question and thereby into a new relationship in which thought and language about God becomes authentic." In order to understand the divine action that results in the human action of thinking about God as he is in himself, we need to understand the nature of that double, metacritical movement which concludes with our being confronted with the presence of God. We have noted how far the critical models of Feuerbach and deconstruction can take us, and we must certainly take them seriously to that extent. But insofar as Feuerbach and deconstruction retreat at last into a religion of the self, we are still confronted with the question as to how thought can maintain the sense of crisis in respect to its thinking about God, so that the reality of God *that thinks itself in our thoughts* may present itself to our thought.

c. *Scharlemann*

In a recent essay entitled "Onto- and Theo-logical Thinking,"[23] Robert Scharlemann, himself a keen student and critic of deconstruction, takes us a bit further. He refuses to let thought of God collapse into thought about the self, and moves forward into the possibility of a *donative* rather than an *assertive* type of thinking that is dependent upon the action of God.

For Scharlemann, as we mentioned earlier, thinking means "to present something to mind as it is on its own."[24] "Thinking" defined in this way may be *objective* thinking in which I not only distinguish, but separate my thought from an object. It may be *reflective* thinking, which brings together thought and objects by way of abstract qualities such as "truth," "beauty," etc., or it may be *reflexive* thinking in which "thought" and "object" are joined. Thinking about thinking, for instance, implies an absolute identity between thinking and the thing thought, because no difference exists between my "thinking" and the "thought" about which I am thinking. According to Scharlemann, thinking about being itself also involves the reflexive mode; unlike "truth" or "beauty" or any other metaphysical idea, "being" represents the underlying reality which constitutes the unity or connection of things. Thus my thinking of being is itself a case of being.

Now if we speak of God as "the ground and power of being," as "being-itself" (Tillich), then as Scharlemann makes clear, theology belongs to the "reflexive" mode in which the thought of God and the reality of God are joined. But care must be taken at this point. If God is "God," his way of being the ground and power of being is necessarily different from any other "ground" or "power." For this reason thought about God (if it is really thought about "God") involves both unity and distinction. Thus Scharlemann asserts that, while thinking about God belongs to the reflexive mode of thought, it is at the same time an *inversion* of that mode. He defines the thinking appropriate to the nature and reality of God in this way: *"to think theologically is to think of the thinking of being (ontology) not as our thinking of being, but as the being*

of God when God is not being God."[25] This formula, the opaqueness
of which is required by its context, might be restated as follows: to
think of God in a way appropriate to his nature requires me to
think of my thinking about God (which is necessarily an
extension of my understanding of being) *not* as my thinking of
God (in that way), but as my thinking of God who engages my
thought in terms of contradiction, that is, in ways which disclose
the fact that God is "different" from my thought.

"To think of our thinking [of God] as not our thinking [of God]"
involves an apophatic[26] turn of mind which Scharlemann calls
"after-thinking" (*meta-noein*).[27] This apophatic and "metanoetic"
thinking places the thinker at risk, because it places the thinker at
the critical juncture where there can be no question of simply
inserting one's own possibilities in the place of God. Here one
thinks "God" as "not thought." For this reason Scharlemann
takes us a considerable way into the metacritical movement
which presents the possibility of authentic thinking about God.

Scharlemann's analysis also evokes the crisis of confrontation
which calls the thinker into question. He speaks of authentic
thought about God as "donative," because it does not arise from
the thinker, but receives what it is told by another — as, for
instance, through the narrative of the gospel. This receptivity
involves a turning around, which the scripture speaks of as
"repentance" (*metanoia*). Authentic thought about God depends
upon an act of God "when God is not being God." That is to say,
when God reveals himself, he necessarily employs finitude
which, as such, is inappropriate for the infinite being of God.
Authentic thinking about God does not dissolve this contradiction. The metacritical situation does not change. The reality
of God available to thought in such a way that it *becomes* our
thought, is at the same time both a disclosure of that reality and a
reminder that it is not our reality.

Scharlemann brings us to the threshold of the last stage of our
consideration of authentic "thinking about God." Here faith must
move beyond the necessary negativity of reflexive thinking about
God to consider how it happens that we do in fact think about
God. The last turn belongs to the metacritical situation which
confronts the thinker with the reality of God by way of narratives
in which God appears as what God is not (e.g., as "king,"
"father," "son of Mary," "the crucified," etc.), or as Moltmann

has observed, faith "must think of the suffering of Christ as the power of God and the death of Christ as God's potentiality."[28] That confrontation involves not only the recognition of the fact that our thought about God can only be of what God is not, but also that, in the event of revelation, even this as "our" thought is replaced and inverted by an act of God which negates the negative and produces the thought of God as what God is. The knowledge and thought of faith, including the ways or analogies by which we think of God, are themselves results of God's own action of self-disclosure. Authentic thinking about God is, therefore, the result of what Barth has called the analogy of faith (*analogia fidei*).

III. Karl Barth and the Analogy of Faith

As Friedrich-Wilhelm Marquardt has reminded us, Barth's early theology took shape in the midst of the struggle for liberation.[29] At first a follower of religious socialism, Barth more and more distanced himself from that movement, because it identified the kingdom of God with a Marxist utopia. Barth remained a socialist, committed to the cause of freedom; but he insisted that God's freedom is more radical than any envisioned by socialism. "The revolutionary has erred: he should really aim at *the* revolution, which is the impossible possibility, the forgiveness of sins, the resurrection of the dead."[30] For Barth, the "revolution of God . . . brings something really new, something which actually transforms the existing order from the ground up."[31] The question for the young Barth was how can theology speak of God in a way that does not confuse God's freedom with the program and goals of this or that revolutionary struggle. Thus it happened that early in his theological career Barth was caught up in what we have described as the first movement of metacriticism. He revolted so strongly against liberal theology's easy identification of God with human knowledge and values, that in the first edition of his famous commentary on Romans he denied *any* legitimacy to human thinking about God. In a sermon from this period he described thinking about God in this way:

> [God is] merely the great solemn word for the unknown, unsearchable reality . . . a beautiful, true thought . . . the

fire . . . next to which we now and then like to warm our
feelings . . . How empty, how weak is the God we have set
up . . . If only God were something besides an idea! . . . Our
beautiful, pious, intelligent ideas of God can go to the devil!
Indeed, aren't they of the devil?"[32]

God is known only because God reveals himself — but for Barth,
God reveals himself as "hidden." The experience of God in
revelation is immediate and momentary: it does not establish an
equivalence between our existence and the existence of God
which allows us to produce a language or thought capable of
grasping that reality. Since, however, religious devotion and
thought necessarily belong to the life of faith, Barth in the second
edition of his *Romans* spoke positively of thought about God —
but only as an "impossible possibility."[33]

> the possibility of clothing the divine in the garment of the
> human, and the eternal in a temporal parable . . . can be
> permitted only when the possibility is recognized as an
> *impossible* possibility. We must not conclude from this that we
> have achieved a secure standing place. We have done no more
> than make room for the "Moment" which has no before and no
> after.[34]

Revelation does not produce an epistemology. That authentic
thinking about God takes place in the moment of God's self-
disclosure does not in itself authorize theology. "As theologians," wrote Barth, "we ought to speak of God. We are human,
however, and so cannot speak of God."[35] Here Barth moves to
the second or metacritical position required about God. He does
not allow any easement of the crisis which thrusts the thinker
before the living God.

For Barth, no ontological connection between divine and
human being could provide the possibility of thinking and
speaking of God. Nor was such a possibility achieved by any
diminution of the absolute difference between the divine and
the human. Rather, that the thought of faith can actually
correspond to its object was found by Barth to depend upon two
things: first, this knowledge of faith depends upon the fact that
the mere existence of God presents itself to our minds by way of
our apprehension of the meaning of the name "God"; and

second, any correspondence between faith and its object
depends upon the perception that the positive content of our
thoughts about God are products of God's own action toward us.
Barth discovered the first of these principles in his study of
Anselm's proof for the existence of God; the second resulted from
it and found expression in his doctrine of the *analogia fidei*.

Barth's 1931 study, *Anselm: Fides Quaerens Intellectum*, allowed
him to move from a purely negative theology to the positive
theology of the *Church Dogmatics*. Through Anselm's proof for
God's existence, Barth discovered a way of thinking about God
which did not deny the contradiction between human thought
and divine being, but precisely on that basis showed how God
could, indeed *must*, be thought to be real.

Anselm's proof (briefly stated) runs thus: (1) everyone, even
the atheist, knows that the name "God" stands for "that than
which a greater cannot be thought,"; (2) the atheist, who knows
this meaning of the *name* "God" but denies that such a being
exists, is caught in a contradiction; (3) because even if one does
not believe or accept that God exists, one can *think* of a God who
exists — and to think of a God who exists means to think of a
greater being than a God who does *not* exist; (4) thus to think of
God as non-existent is impossible, since from the first even the
atheist admits that "God" means "that than which a greater
cannot be thought."

Insofar as philosophy has sought in this proof a logic which
establishes the existence of God, it has, according to Barth, badly
misread Anselm. For the proof, as Anselm himself put it, is an
attempt at "understanding" (*intelligere*) that *presupposes* the reality
of God and the gracious action of God toward human being and
human thought. For this reason the argument begins with a
prayer of illumination and closes with this prayer of thanksgiv-
ing:

> I thank thee, good Lord, I thank thee, that what I first believed
> because of thy gift, I now know because of thine illumining in
> such a way that even if I did not want to believe thine existence,
> yet I could not but know it.[36]

So Anselm's proof must be viewed as a theological and not a
philosophical exercise, because it not only assumes the reality of

God, but assumes as well a continuing relationship with God which empowers any legitimate thinking about God.

For Barth, Anselm's proof provided a specific answer to the question of how thinking about God can be legitimate in face of the fact that we have no capacity for such thought. Anselm's argument turns on the famous phrase "that than which a greater cannot be thought." Only because of the way we *cannot* think of God (that there could be a "greater") do we discover that we *must* think of God (as existing, as "God"). God acts and decides in the pure aseity of the divine freedom to be "that than which no greater can be thought," and in that way attaches to every thought about the name "God," the prohibition that another could be conceived as greater. As Barth comments, "God himself compels this knowledge . . . Wherever God has been known, he himself has excluded the very thought of [his non-existence] with mathematical precision."[37]

We cannot underscore too strongly the point that legitimate thought about God comes about by a sustained metacritical attitude which recognizes the incapacity of human thought about God and throws the thinker into the crisis where God's prior act and thought displaces our thought about God. This act of God's self-disclosure to our thought completes the metacritical movement of faith.

The possibility Barth found in Anselm of thinking and speaking legitimately about God enabled him to move from a theology of crisis to a theology capable of dogmatic construction. If the self-disclosing action of God empowers thought to think the reality of God, then that same revelatory activity may enable us to think not only of the mere existence of God, but also of God's character and attributes, of his freedom in himself and for us that alone inspires and empowers true liberation. For this reason Eberhard Jüngel characterizes Barth's study of Anselm as a move from dialectical opposition to analogy.[38]

To speak of thought and knowledge is necessarily to speak of analogy. Medieval theologies under the influence of Plato and Aristotle conceived of God as belonging to the totality of being, and therefore in some sense "like" other being. By an analogy based upon the connectedness of being (*analogia entis*) they could account for thought and knowledge of God. Barth was an avowed enemy of such natural theology and the *analogia entis* upon which it is based. But even for Barth, there must exist some enabling connection between human thought and God if theological thinking is to be authentic. The connection, however, is not one naturally and universally inherent because humans exist and God exists — and share the common attribute of "being." The being of God is not like our being. The analogy that creates the possibility of our thinking and knowing God is therefore an analogy produced by the specific act of God. Such an analogy is called by Barth an *analogia fidei* (analogy of faith), or sometimes an *analogia gracie* or *analogia attributionis*, because the connection and similarity achieved are, like faith itself, wholly the responsibility of God and the result of his gracious decision and act alone. Of course, as in the relation of faith, we too have a part. We must respond and believe. Thus, in the analogies made possible by faith we may think and speak of God, clothing the divine in human garment. We do so, however, as in faith, dependent at every point upon the priority of God's thought to our own — and attentive to the difference.

If we ask how it happens that our thinking about God can really become analogous to the reality of God, Barth answers in the following way. At the critical juncture where we encounter revelation, language and thought are "drawn into the darkness and light of its mystery."[39] That human speech should in this way be drawn into the divine word depends upon the Word made flesh: "Jesus Christ himself sees to it."[40] As he did once for all in the Christ, so in ever different ways God, in unimaginable freedom, really "makes himself the object of our cognition."[41] This action of God, whereby we are enabled to think of God, involves "no magical transformation of man or supernatural enlargement of his capacity," for in respect to our ability to think of God, "[we] cannot do it afterward any more than [we] could do it before."[42] Where thinking about God confronts both human incapacity and God's grace it becomes obvious that although we cannot appropriate God in our thought, God "will appropriate us, and in so doing *permit* and *command* and therefore *adapt* us to appropriate him."[43] Just as the human words of the Bible may become the Word of God, so too the thinking that belongs to faith can actually coincide with the truth of God. "God's true revelation comes from out of itself to meet what we can say with our human words and makes a selection from among them to which we have to attach ourselves in obedience."[44] But because this is the result of God's action, it can never become the basis of any claim that our thoughts and words bear an univocal or equivocal relation to the being of God. There can only be an analogy which God controls, "elevating our words to their proper use, giving himself to be their proper object, and therefore giving them truth."[45]

The recovery of the freedom of God for human liberation requires that we learn again to think of our thinking of God in this way. Only in this way can we really think of God as *God* — as God is free in himself and thereby able to be free for us in Jesus Christ, inspiring and enabling human liberation.

God reaches out to human thought and language primarily and authoritatively through scripture which, as human thought, is nonetheless the free and liberating word of a free and liberating God — and to that topic we must now turn.

4

The Liberating Word

Introduction

If the possibility of thinking and speaking of the liberating freedom of God is not our own, if *our* words cannot in themselves be the liberating word of God, then we must seek that word where it is found, hear it where it is spoken, and read it where it is written. We must again heed the advice of Calvin — "*Ad verbum est veniendum*" ("You must come to the word") — by which he meant the written words of the Bible.[1]

I did not intend, when I first titled the lecture which stands behind this chapter, to use the title of an early (1976) book edited by Letty Russell. I am glad, however, to acknowledge the indebtedness, for at the beginning and end of her *The Liberating Word* Russell writes:

> The Word of God is living and liberating to those who hear with faith and live it out in faith . . . The liberating Word is the power of the gospel to renew our lives continually, opening them to freedom and future. It is important to guard the power of that original story against distortion and not to write into it our own limited perspectives . . . It is not necessary to rewrite or add to the Bible . . . The Bible is a witness to the promise that God continues to be with us as Creator, Liberator, and Advocate.[2]

The question as to whether Professor Russell now finds these earlier views entirely congenial need not detain us or distract us from attending to the two major points she has raised: that the Bible is the liberating word of God, and that it must not be confused with any other words that we might rather read or hear.

The Freedom of the Word

When we speak of the freedom of God's word, we must begin with the Word of God itself, the *logos* that became flesh in Jesus Christ. This eternal "Word of God" has the same freedom as God has in himself, because as the Gospel of John puts it, this Word which "became flesh and dwelt among us, full of grace and truth," "was in the beginning with God" (John 1:14, 2). So the Word of God is free, free to create in the beginning, free to save in the human life of the Son, and free to liberate the daughters and sons of God through the presence of the Spirit.

As human language written, the Bible is not free in the same way that the Word of God itself is free. But in so far as the written words of the Bible bear witness to God's liberating power, they too are free and liberating — and liberating because they are free. To speak of the freedom and liberating power of the biblical word is, therefore, to speak of a derivative and secondary, but no less real, freedom and liberation. Because God speaks through this written word, we may discover a correspondence between the way the Bible is free and the way that God is free. In terms of the fourfold structure of divine freedom, we can say that, as God is free *for* us, free *in* himself, free *from* other being and free also *from* his ways of being *for* us, so there are in scripture corresponding forms of freedom.[3]

I. The Freedom of the Word For Us

Just as the other forms of divine freedom must be understood first in terms of God's freedom for us, so too reflection upon the freedom of the word must begin at the same place. God's freedom for us confronts us in the Word made flesh, and there can be no other form of the word of God, nor any freedom of that word for us, that does not correspond to Jesus Christ. This means that the freedom of the written word finds expression in its incarnational character.

That there exists a correspondence between the written words of scripture and the incarnate word, Jesus Christ, has long been known in theology. For Luther, the Bible "contains" or "holds" the living word as, to use his famous simile, the cradle held the infant Jesus. "Here you will find the swaddling cloths and the manger in which Christ lies, and to which the angel points the shepherds. Simple and lowly are these swaddling cloths, but dear is the treasure, Christ, who lies in them."[4]

Calvin brings out a similar correspondence between the written and incarnate word when he speaks of both as "mirrors" reflecting the will of God.[5] The words of scripture represent, as does the humanity of Christ, an "accommodation" of God to our fleshly existence and need. "For the Lord knows quite well," wrote Calvin, "that if he were to speak to us in a manner befitting his majesty, our intelligence would be incapable of reaching that high. Thus he accommodates himself to our smallness. And as a wet-nurse coos to its baby, so he uses toward us an unrefined way of speaking in order to be understood."[6]

Karl Barth gave the greatest emphasis to this connection. According to Barth, Calvin's comment that "salvation resides in his flesh"[7] refers also to the presence of God in the human words of the Bible's prophets and apostles. Of course there is a difference between the incarnation and biblical testimony. There is no unity of persons between God and those writers, nor can their words independently reveal. They can only attest the revelation in Christ. And yet Barth claims that "as the witness of witnesses directly called in and with revelation itself, scripture too stands in that indirect identity of human existence with God himself, which is occasioned neither by the nature of God nor that of man, but brought about by the decision and act of God."[8]

We have said that the incarnation expresses God's *freedom* for us. In what way does it do this? As *kenosis*, as an "emptying" or accommodation, the incarnation displays the freedom of God, and does so not merely as a self-inflicted sacrifice, restriction, and suffering which God undertakes on our behalf. It was that, of course, but it was also an appropriate and even necessary expression of God's freedom. In God's becoming something other and lower than himself, God actually exercises and demonstrates divine freedom. In a sense this had to take place, for as Barth writes, "if he wished to reveal himself, if he wished to be free for us, this very miracle had to take place, namely, that without ceasing to be himself he entered our sphere, assumed our nature."[9] The same is true for scripture. Some believe that endowing biblical language with the divine perfection of inerrancy enhances its freedom and power. Such a view, however, is docetic and denies the freedom of the word by denying its capacity to take on human form. As God discloses his freedom and power by becoming human in Christ, so too the freedom of the word finds expression in its concrete and limited humanity.

We might wish it otherwise. We might want the Bible free of temporal limitation, the better to express timeless truth. We might wish that, in respect to its ethics, the Old Testament contained none of the sanctified violence and ancient prejudice that scar its texts. We cannot, however, increase the freedom of the word to address the human condition by depriving the Bible of its finite and human character. To the contrary, we thereby deny the freedom of God to do so, for it is exactly the problematic humanity of the biblical text (what Ernst Käsemann calls "the practical and mundane" dimension) that makes its cause "the cause of freedom."[10] For this reason we cannot possibly agree with the "critical principle," enunciated by Rosemary Ruether in *Sexism and God-Talk*, that in the Bible "whatever denies, diminishes, or distorts the full humanity of women" cannot be included in "the authentic message of redemption."[11] Such an approach forfeits the liberating power of the Bible by rejecting the fallible human character of scripture that shows it to be the free word of a free God *for* us.

II. The Freedom of the Word in Itself

Now we turn to the primary form of divine freedom, namely, the freedom of God in himself. We have already shown that under this form of God's freedom we encounter the absolute otherness of God. Of course, the Bible in itself is not free in this way. As a human text it is contingent. Far from being self-caused, the Bible is the result of a constellation of causes. The various narratives in the Bible are inextricably tied to their own contexts and are therefore limited to the knowledge and values of their time. How, then, can we claim for the Bible *any* correspondence to the primary freedom of God in himself?

The answer lies in what earlier Reformed theologians called the self-authentication of scripture. Calvin writes: "The testimony of the Spirit is more excellent than all reason. For God alone is a fit witness of himself in his Word . . . Scripture is indeed self-authenticated; hence it is not right to subject it to proof and reasoning . . . For even if it wins reverence for itself by its own majesty, it seriously affects us only when it is sealed upon our hearts through the Spirit."[12] The Second Helvetic and Westminster Confessions testify similarly to the inner authority of scripture.[13] The inner freedom of the Bible to authenticate itself is, therefore, not really its own freedom, but a freedom given it by what earlier theologians called "the internal testimony of the Holy Spirit."

What can be observed in scripture that illustrates this self-authentication through the Spirit? In the first place, as the witness to the Word of God made flesh in Jesus Christ, the Bible makes its whole concern the word of God, that is, the reality of God and the meaning of God for human life. Even on the outer edges of its narrative, where genealogies, cultic law, sensuous poetry, or apocalyptic visions may obscure that word of God, it can still be heard.

In the second place, the Bible does not confuse its own witness and thought with the reality and thought of God. For Barth, the Bible is like the "prodigious" finger of John the Baptist in Grünewald's "Crucifixion" — pointing away from itself toward the Christ.

> Can anyone point to the thing indicated more impressively and realistically than is done there? . . . Why and in what respect does the biblical witness possess authority? In that it claims no authority whatsoever for itself, that its witness amounts to letting the [word, revelation itself] be the authority.[14]

Confirming this interpretation of Grünewald's portrayal of John, the critic Geoffery Harpham argues that John's finger and the slogan written above his arm ("He must increase, but I must decrease") represent Grünewald's personal attitude toward the whole work — which is illustrated by the artist himself in his refusal to sign the painting.[15] This biographical note serves to underline the theological point. The Baptist as precursor of the Word, the Bible as the written word, and the painter as the (artistic) preacher of the word, fulfill their function only as they point away from themselves to what Barth has called "the something else." Similarly, Paul Tillich has argued that biblical faith is an adequate medium of revelation because, in the Old Testament, the "concrete" expression of God in Israel is not identified with "the name of his nation and its particular qualities."[16] In the New Testament the medium of revelation (the man Jesus) is sacrificed to its substance (the Logos). "A revelation is final if it has the power of negating itself without losing itself."[17] For Tillich, it is the human, self-critical, and self-negating character of the Bible that makes it an adequate medium of revelation.

The Bible thus manifests its inner authenticity by the consistency of its reference to something other than itself. As a written word, it does not identify itself with the living Word of God. The Bible maintains the distinction between its own humanity and the reality of God by eschewing any attempt to achieve consistency or other perfection of its texts. A levitical religion of cult and temple is allowed to stand side by side with a prophetic faith which can only "hate and despise . . . feasts and solemn assemblies" (Amos 5:22). Nor is that prophetic protest later overturned by the quite opposite interests of Ezra-Nehemiah.

Because the word of God participates in the freedom of God, it is an effective instrument of God's liberating power. In and through its texts the Bible proclaims a divine revolution in human affairs, a liberation from everything that oppresses human life. God opens a limitless horizon of possibility to Abraham and Sarah and their descendants. In the Mosaic stories God makes good on those promises by liberating the chosen people from political oppression through the exodus and from the self-inflicted oppression of sin through Torah. God's deliverance of his people from oppression becomes the dominant theme in the time of the two kingdoms, and even more so during the exile and return. Under the prophets the ultimate eschatological freedom promised by God is coupled with the demand that the people of Israel serve the cause of liberation by dealing with one another in justice and peace. This theme continues into the New Testament where the fulfillment of human liberation appears in Jesus Christ, who "put down the mighty from their thrones and exalted those of high degree" (Luke 1:51–54). Those who want a share in that future freedom must themselves take part in the present struggle. It will not be a question of who says "Lord, Lord," but of who is engaged in the revolutionary praxis of God's will — to wit, those who feed "my sheep," clothe the naked, and help those in prison (Matt. 25:31).

There can be no doubt that the Bible speaks a liberating word effectively and in power. The disclosure of the liberating power to Paul's Philippian jailer (Acts 16:25ff.) was but a foretaste of what the word of God would accomplish among the oppressed classes of Rome, Saxon peasants in the sixteenth century, German Christians at Barmen, blacks in the United States and South Africa, Catholic Poles under communism, and South Americans threatened by North American intervention.

Any experience of the liberating power of scripture, however, requires a recognition of the freedom given it by the freedom of God. If we do not recognize this freedom of the word, the Bible may direct our attention to the highest religious and social ideals, but we will miss its liberating power. It is, therefore, of great importance for the cause of liberation that, as the word of God, the Bible be understood as properly free in itself. This principle must become the prior and overarching hermeneutic of liberation theology. What does it mean to speak of the inner freedom of scripture as a "hermeneutic"? It means to approach the Bible with the expectation that in it we will hear the liberating word of God in power and *in its own way*. Of course, we need other principles as well. The hermeneutic of suspicion so often evoked in feminist theology is absolutely necessary, because it reveals the radical humanness of the Bible against which the radical freedom of the word of God is displayed. Jon Sobrino's "hermeneutic of revolutionary praxis"[18] and Gustavo Gutiérrez's "political" hermeneutic[19] help keep in view the freedom of the word in discipleship and liberating service. For Gutiérrez, however, a policital hermeneutic ought not to contradict the inner freedom of scripture. For Gutiérrez, while we must undertake

> a re-reading of the gospel from a position of solidarity with the poor . . . this will be grasped in all its implications only if we are conscious of the ongoing creative and critical character of the gospel's liberating message. For the gospel . . . can never be identified with any concrete social formula, however just that formula may seem to us at the moment.[20]

The inner creative and critical freedom of the word provides a proto-hermeneutic by which may be avoided the Scylla and Charybdis of contemporary political theology, namely, the tendency to associate human freedom with the bankrupt theories of Marxism-Leninism *or* the equally hopeless (and today possibly more dangerous) assumptions of modern capitalism. To suggest a prior hermeneutic of self-authentication does not deny, but gives needed support and direction to, the principles of interpretation already employed in liberation theology.

Such is the meaning of the inner freedom of the word which corresponds to the freedom that God has within himself. But now let us turn to the two other forms of that freedom—God's freedom *from* other being, and God's freedom *from* the various ways he is free *for* us — and see how these find expression in the Bible.

III. The Freedom of the Word From Other Being

The self-authenticating, inner freedom that scripture receives by virtue of the action of God means that its witness is also free *from* the contingencies that control other ideas, language, and texts. When from time to time the Bible becomes the word of God, it is delivered from the nexus of cause and effect that determines all other texts. If this were not the case, the Bible could not be liberating. If it were simply and without exception bound to its own time, it would be no more compelling for human justice and peace than the Magna Carta or the United States Constitution, and in fact would probably be less so. In contrast to other writing, the Bible as employed by the word of God is freed from the concepts and values of its authors—concepts the best of which were limited and the worst of which were vicious. We have already called attention to this form of biblical freedom when we noted that, in spite of the indisputable racism, sexism, and violence that informs much of scripture, it has nonetheless proven to be *the* liberating word in human history.

If, in its function of attestation and witness, the Bible displays a freedom from the prejudices that informed its original authorship, it also proves itself free from the values and presuppositions that we attempt to impose upon it. Such imposition takes many forms, but always involves a desire to perfect the Bible, to make it more "literally" correct. Thus, in one way or another, such attempts display the underlying tendency of fundamentalism. In a joint article written in 1888, A. A. Hodge and B. B. Warfield summarized a fundamentalist doctrine of infallibility in the following way:

All the affirmations of Scripture of all kinds, whether of spiritual doctrine or duty, or of physical or historical fact, or of psychological or philosophical principle, are without any error, when the *ipsissima verba* of the original autographs are ascertained and interpreted in their natural and intended use.[21]

While this doctrine was meant to secure the authority of scripture, the argument by which it was achieved produced the opposite result. According to Hodge and Warfield, we must "first establish Theism, then the historical credibility of Scriptures, and *then* the divine origin of Christianity."[22]

This means that whatever else the word of God may be, it is not the primary source of the knowledge of God; nor is the action of God through the Holy Spirit fundamental to the Bible's authority. That authority depends rather upon what they called the Bible's "historical credibility," which cannot be discovered in the text itself but from what can be "ascertained" from original autographs. Although these original autographs have not in the providence of God been preserved in the church, the "thoughts and words" contained in them were supposed by Hodge and Warfield to have been miraculously protected from error by "divine superintendence."[23]

Here, then, is a doctrine which radically denies the indispensable freedom and authority of scripture. For what freedom can scripture have if its primary authority is co-opted by a theism obtained from Scottish Realism or some other philosophy?[24] What authority can be assigned to the Bible, if that authority depends upon an "historical credibility" — which must be "ascertained" from original autographs which are themselves *un*ascertainable? Does not such a logic render the Bible *in*credible? The intention of Warfield and Hodge was benign, but the effect was disastrous. What was intended as a service to the Bible turned out to be an attempt to master it by a theory that denied its humanity. They did not see that, as God is free for us in Jesus Christ, so is his word free for us in the humanity of its authorship. Thus they in fact rejected the word of God given to the church by attempting to correct it by what they considered a better word of their own invention and imagination.

I have raised the issue of biblical fundamentalism not because modern theology is apt to adopt its substance, but because we are in danger of accepting its perspective and method. For instance, Elizabeth Schüssler Fiorenza in her book, *Bread Not Stone: The Challenge of Feminist Biblical Interpretation*, employs Ricoeur's distinction between an "archaeological" and a "teleological" interpretation of literature to discover a world of meaning in *front* of the biblical text. Armed with this hermeneutic, Schüssler Fiorenza can recognize the Bible's androcentrism, set it aside, and replace it with a reconstructed history of women in the primitive church. The underlying principle of this hermeneutic can also be seen in her earlier book, *In Memory of Her*, where it is claimed that "biblical revelation and truth are given only in those texts . . . that transcend critically their patriarchal frameworks."[25] Because Professor Schüssler Fiorenza does not see that the free word of God is able to liberate *all* biblical texts from patriarchy (and worse), she is left with mere fragments of the New Testament narrative able to meet her test. And so, like Warfield and Hodge, she must propose an imaginary and more perfect text produced by a "hermeneutics of remembrance and historical reconstruction"[26] as the real word of God which, upon her own account, amounts to a new apocrypha. "Such a retelling of biblical stories is not a feminist invention. Throughout the centuries we have examples of parallel elaborations such as the apocryphal infancy stories of our Christmas legends."[27]

This essentially fundamentalist desire to correct and master the written word of God by perfecting its language can also be seen in *The Inclusive Language Lectionary*, published in 1983 by the National Council of Churches in the United States.[28] In these altered readings from the Bible we have the ultimate expression of every theory of inerrancy, which Paul Lehmann describes as "a recrudescence of the lamentable textual literalism which has contributed its own share to the loss and violation of God's name. The crusaders for pro-nominal equivocity [are] like their fundamentalistic predecessors and contemporaries who relentlessly insist upon univocity."[29] The major difference between fundamentalism and the *Inclusive Language Lectionary* is that the former merely asserts the Bible's perfection, while the latter attempts to achieve it by overt correction of the text.[30] Such corrections take place in the *Lectionary* on three different levels. First, the *Lectionary* corrects androcentric references to God by substituting "Sovereign" for "Lord," and adding to every reference to God as "Father" the phrase "*and Mother.*"[31] Second, it corrects the androcentric history of the Bible by creating references to females wherever possible. Thus, to every formulaic reference to Abraham is added "*and Sarah,*" and to epistolary references to "brethren" is attached "and sisters," etc.[32] Finally and most astonishingly, other changes are made, not because the text is considered wrong in fact or intention, but because the editors believe their emendations will better serve the cause of inclusiveness. Thus the "watchman" in Ezek. 33:2 is changed to "watcher," and (*mirabile dictu!*) Mary gives birth to a "firstborn child" — of indeterminate sex.[33]

This frontal assault upon the Bible cannot be blamed upon Ricoeur, Gadamer, or even Derrida, none of whom ever suggested that a historic text be *changed* to fit the views of the reader. One can only express puzzlement that scholars with historical and philological responsibilities could tolerate (much less participate in) such barbaric treatment of the Jewish and Christian scriptures. In the words of Paul Minear, "to alter the thoughts, intention, and language of the Bible [is] a covert but nonetheless destructive repudiation of the authority of the Bible over the church."[34] But however serious its threat to culture, however absurd it may render biblical scholarship, the really dangerous thing about *The Inclusive Language Lectionary* is that it not only ignores the freedom and integrity of the word of God, but in fact removes that word from the community of faith.[35] It abandons the free and liberating word of God in favour of human language which is neither free nor liberating—and that is bad news for the cause of human liberation in general and for women's liberation in particular.

The Bible ever again proves itself free from all such attempts to master and correct its content and message. It shows itself free equally from its own errors and our corrections by bearing witness to the liberating power of God. The Bible needs no improvement from literalism, old or new.[36] As witness to the Word, the words of the Bible possess the necessary freedom to be self-corrective. This is the final form of the Bible's freedom, which corresponds to the structure of God's own freedom.

IV. The Freedom of the Word As Self-Correction

Although God's freedom for us always offers grace, mercy, and salvation, God is not captive to particular methods and forms of his grace. The liberating power of God always takes new and unexpected forms. God works in all sorts of ways which have little to do with what we might expect from either scripture or human history. The God who spoke through Balaam's ass can speak through a fundamentalist, a feminist hermeneutic — or a theological essay. The Lord God of Hosts can change the course of history through a defeated nation or a defeated bunch of *campacinos* in Latin America. Nothing is absolutely predictable. In the past, Chinese students as "Red Guards" assaulted faith and terrorized their neighbors in the name of proletarian dictatorship; more recently, they sacrificed themselves for the freedom of others. When the power of the state seems most invincible, it can happen that, in the providence of God, one lone man stands up for all and stops a column of tanks in Tiananmen Square. When believers fail, God is quite able to use unbelievers — new Cyruses — to bring about justice and peace.[37] Such a freedom from what (from our point of view) must be expected is an essential element of the meaning of God's freedom for human liberation.

In its human, biblical form, the word is not free in the same way that God is free. It is, however, free in ways that correspond to God's freedom. This means that, as God is free to alter and even reverse his ways of being for us, so in scripture we find this same kind of freedom in the form of self-correction. We have above written some harsh words about those who attempt to correct scripture. In what way then does scripture correct itself? Such inner correction will not take the form of one or another perfection of its texts, rendering it without error. As we have seen, any such perfection would deny the Bible's humanity. Such a denial would not be a correction but the self-destruction of the Bible, because when the Bible is employed as a witness, it is precisely the fallibility of its human words that demonstrate the absolute freedom of God.

The self-correction of scripture is manifest whenever the limitation of its human form is overcome without denying that form. In ever-changing contexts, the Bible directs our attention to other meanings in its text which shed new light on old meanings redeeming them for the gospel of God.[38] In the period of the Exodus the liberating word of God had to be heard in terms of patriarchal and tribal cult. During the monarchy a national temple cult was needed — just as later, during the divided kingdom, a prophetic vision of God's universality began to appear. So it goes throughout the Old and New Testaments as God's word parallels and demonstrates God's freedom from his prior ways of being free for his people.

Furthermore, because scripture bears witness to the fact that no human word can itself be the word of God, we find in the Bible something like a self-deconstruction. What Derrida calls a reversal of assumed polarities (good/bad, clean/unclean, male/female, etc.) may also be seen in scripture. Jesus "came not to call the righteous, but sinners;" (Matt. 9:13, Mark 2:17); the "first will be last, and the last first" (Matt. 19:30). The relation between the clean and unclean is reversed (Matt. 3:27–28) by one in whom "there is neither male nor female" (Gal. 3:28). Also, like other deconstructed text, the Bible discloses insignificant bits of text that "give the game away," denying what otherwise seems affirmed.[39] In the patriarchal narratives, for instance, Phyllis Trible finds the marginal person Hagar to represent a more significant witness to God's mysterious and even terrifying "otherness" than either Abraham or Sarah.

Perhaps the best illustration of the Bible's metacritical self-correction may be found in its notorious application of gender to God. That such references arise out of patriarchal co-optation of the name and image of God cannot be denied in light of the pervasive and oppressive androgyny of the canon. Nor can it be denied that in the church male pride and presumption has all too willingly adopted this usage, and in doing so, made itself liable to the warning of Luther that God holds in judgment "those pot-bellies" and "high and mighty" who violate God's name.[40] Yet in scripture itself, this chauvinism becomes subject to clear and consistent criticism, as for instance, in the first and second commandments and in such prophetic declarations as "I am God and not man, the Holy One in your midst" (Hos. 11:9;. The Old Testament's refusal to apply male sexual activity to God likewise indicates the Bible's absolute rejection of what its metaphoric language about God might otherwise indicate.[41]

If chauvinism in scripture and the church has created a situation which in some sense justifies Mary Daly's famous dictum, "Since God is male, the male is God,"[42] it is equally true that both the premise and conclusion of that statement are denied in scripture itself. If we fail to see this and suppose that the Bible needs correction on this point, we will only "double the negative" and negate the judgment that scripture has already lodged against the projection of maleness upon God.

The addition of female imagery to scripture betrays both a literary and theological misunderstanding of the way the biblical text works. Roland Frye argues that, among other things, the imposition of female imagery upon the Bible's portrayal of the divine image arises from a failure to note the different meanings conveyed by similes and metaphors. "In feminist interpretation, simile and metaphor are confused and even conflated so that a simile is assumed to do what a metaphor is in fact designed to do. Whereas similes compare, metaphors predicate or name."[43] According to Frye, when the Bible uses similes to speak of God "*as* a woman in travail" or "*like* an eagle," a different kind of description is intended from that provided by metaphors such as "God the Father," "Christ the Son," Jesus "the Lamb," etc. Similes "illustrate some phase of divine attitude or intent" but are not "transparent to personal identity as are predicating metaphors."[44] Thus it is a mistake when Virginia Mollenkott exuberantly twists the comparison into an identification by declaring that "God is our mother-eagle."[45] While from our perspective (as outlined in the previous chapter) metaphors are no more (or, as witnesses, no less) "transparent" to divinity than are similes, the literary, functional difference presented by Professor Frye ought to be observed in any translation and interpretation of the Bible. From the perspective of the doctrine of scripture presented here, one might say that the Bible is equally self-critical and self-corrective in respect to both similes and metaphors. The difference is that the simile contains in itself the corrective ("as," "like," etc.), while metaphors require interpretation and correction from other texts. Moses' claim that "The Lord is a man of war" (Exod. 15:3) must be confronted by Balaam's reminder that "God is not a man" (Num. 23:19).

When we try to correct or improve the biblical text we may find ourselves unwittingly affirming what we want to deny. As Paul Hanson has observed, this very thing happens when *The Inclusive Language Lectionary* corrects John the Baptist's attack upon the Pharisees in Matthew 3. The text reads in part, "You brood of vipers . . . do not presume to say to yourselves, 'We have

Abraham as our father,' for I tell you God is able from these stones to raise up children of Abraham" (Matt. 3:9). The lectionary's correction, which renders the words of the Pharisees, "We have Abraham as our father and Sarah and Hagar as our mothers," negates John's rebuke against precisely the patriarchal pride which the lectionary rightly abhors. By adding female to male imagery in the passage the lectionary actually reduplicates the error that John condemns.[46]

The same issue confronts us with Jesus' "father" name for God. Here, too, the Bible leads us away from false conclusions concerning its own language. As Barth pointed out long ago, the "son" and "father" of the New Testament

> do not first and properly have their truth at the point of reference to . . . the two nearest male members in the succession of physical generation . . . [but rather] on the basis of the grace of the revelation of God, they may refer [to] . . . the doctrine of the trinity . . . Their proper use obviously consists in the fact that they point away and beyond themselves, taking on a new pregnancy, referring to that to which they cannot refer at all as our views and concepts.[47]

On this point Professor Schüssler Fiorenza agrees with Barth. "Jesus uses the 'father' name of God not as a legitimation for existing patriarchal power structures in society or church but as a critical subversion of all structures of domination."[48] The critique of the father image in Matthew 23 ("call no one father among you on earth, for you have only one heavenly father") allows, according to Paul Lehmann, the image of God as "father" to point to the "liberating human experience of utter dependence upon the utterly dependable."[49] So not only is there no need for correction of (or liturgical departure from) the text, but there is every reason to take seriously and to use the quite different interpretation the Bible itself wishes to give to God as "father."

The liberating word of the Bible is free for us because, as empowered by God, it is free from every limitation imposed upon it by its own necessary humanity. The Bible is also free equally from our misinterpretation, co-optation, and correction. Where the freedom of the word is seen, where it is read in this light, *we* are liberated from the oppression of human presumption and the spiritual stultification of our own corrections.

Faithful explication of this free word of a free God requires a liberated and liberating theology.

5

Liberating Theology

Introduction

God is free in himself. We are attempting to recover this truth for the cause of liberation, because only on this basis can we know that God is free also from the constraints of nature and history and thus free for the world and able to redeem it. If God is free *in* himself and *from* other being, and free *for* us in Jesus Christ, then Christian theology must itself be liberating. God's concern must be its concern. Christian theology must, in the words of Gustavo Gutiérrez, be "a theology [engaged] in the protest against trampled human dignity, in the struggle against the plunder of the vast majority of people, in liberating love, and in the building of a new, just, and fraternal society."[1]

We can here state only in broad terms the political agenda of a liberating theology — an end to bellicose activity in South America, a renewal of the struggle for racial equality in the West, a reaffirmation of a feminism whose goal is partnership, a search for new strategies for justice in South Africa and China, and a way to encourage the democratization of Eastern Europe and the Soviet Union while avoiding the evils of laissez faire capitalism. The list is extensive, and specific instruction as to means and ends will best come from those on the firing line. At this point our interest is not so much "what" theology must say and do in respect to various liberation contexts, but under what conditions it can say anything at all. The point I want to develop is that theology cannot articulate the gospel in the service of human liberation unless it, too, is liberated from the compulsions that inhibit its faithfulness to that cause.

I. Two Requirements for a Liberating Theology

In light of all that has been said about the freedom of God and the vocation of theology, we may clear some ground by stating two requirements for a liberating theology.

In the first place, a theology concerned with the liberating power of God must be committed to and involved in the struggle for liberation. A liberating theology cannot be merely academic. This point may appear irrelevant, because doctrinal catechesis is already neglected in the parish, prohibited in American public schools, and generally avoided in undergraduate and (even) divinity schools. But however much we may need theological instruction, it must not control the motivation of a liberating theology. The business of such a theology is not primarily the teaching of catechumens, the intellectual edification of undergraduates, or the preparation of seminarians for ordination examinations. Even less, we might add, is it the business of dogmatics to provide a final confessional polish to a ministerial education generally devoid of theological interest — as happens, for instance, when theological curricula place the study of doctrine on the margin of so-called practical theological courses. A theology responsive to the free word of a free God must serve the cause of liberation by explicating the meaning of the freedom of God for the deliverance of the oppressed.

In the second place, a theology directed by the liberating will of God must bind itself to the revelation of that will in Jesus Christ. Such a theology cannot be merely speculative. This point was brought home to me years ago in Basel when I was assigned to report to Barth's seminar on the section "The Determination of the Rejected" in his doctrine of election (*CD* 2.2). I decided to compare Barth's long excursus on Judas with the interpretation of Judas by his father and other representatives of the historical-critical school. I played the devil's advocate. I raised all kinds of historical questions. I was even reckless enough to ask whether, given the length of Barth's treatment, "less" might not have been "more"! The evening was a disaster. Barth sucked discontentedly on his pipe, my attempts at humor fell flat, and my student colleagues, sensing an early end to a doctoral career, would not say a word. A few days later I went with some trepidation to

Barth's house to deliver a chapter of my dissertation and was ushered up to his study by a worried Fraulein von Kirschbaum. Almost before I sat down Barth said, "I could hardly sleep at all the other night. What was going on in that report of yours?" I explained that I thought it would be "interesting" to take the historical critics' perspective. To which Barth exclaimed, "But that's not *your* perspective! Never do that! We don't have time for 'armchair theology!'"

The issue, of course, was not the validity of historical criticism, but the seriousness that ought to accompany theological work. When we are presented, on the one hand, with the concrete reality of the liberating power of God in Jesus Christ, and on the other, with the desperate need of those who are oppressed, is it permissible for theology to be distracted from that reality and need by a theology of "play" or "the goddess" or "the death of God" or any other of the various forms of "armchair theology"?

A theology attentive to the liberating power of God will be a theology that keeps before it the reality of God in Jesus Christ. It will recall that "For freedom Christ has set us free" (Gal. 5:1), and will therefore attend to its task. It may not be a "theology of liberation." Its time and place may not call it to a concentration on Christian praxis in the face of particular oppression, but it will be of service to those that are. Leonardo and Clodovis Boff have observed that "professional" theology engages in study and writing while "pastoral" and "popular" theology address more practical and everyday concerns. However, "each of these levels reflects the *same thing*: faith confronted with oppression, and each . . . reflects this faith *in its own way*."[2] Even as dogmatics, theological work may be decisive for liberation thought and action. Calvin's theology of the sovereign freedom of God inspired two centuries of struggle for religious freedom in Europe and the New World. Barth's dogmatics found concrete application against Nazi tyranny at Barmen, and the connection Paul Lehmann has shown between biblical theology and radical politics has borne fruit in the writings of such South African theologians as Allan Boesak and Charles Villa-Vicencio.[3]

Examples of formal theologies that have contributed to the struggle for liberation could be extended to reveal surprising instances where, as Calvin put it, "God wonderfully preserves his church, as it were in hiding places."[4] For instance, however

much we may object to Benjamin Warfield's doctrine of inerrancy, we ought not to forget that what he understood about
the freedom of God put him miles ahead of the majority of his
Presbyterian contemporaries on issues of justice and equality. In
1888 he stated that the "missionary spirit [must] serve as the hand
of the most high in elevating the lowly and rescuing the
oppressed."[5] In the decades following the American Civil War,
Warfield warned that the Presbyterian church should not be
"willing to buy reunion with its [white] southern brethren at the
fearful cost of affixing an unjust stigma" to blacks.[6]

A liberating theology will not be merely instructive or speculative, but will keep ever in view its primary vocation — the
explication of the gospel of Christ the Liberator.

II. The Freedom of Theology

Liberating theology may turn up in unexpected places, but
whatever form it takes, it will demonstrate that it has been "freed
for freedom." It will be liberating because it has been liberated for
God's cause.

In what sense is a liberating theology free? It would certainly be
architecturally useful for this chapter if we could apply the
fourfold freedom of God to theology as we did to scripture.
Earlier, we proposed a correspondence between the freedom of
God and the freedom of the word. We said that the Bible is free in
itself, is self-authenticating, because even as a human word, the
Bible is also God's word — when and where God employs it in
that way. We cannot, however, say the same of theology, not
even the most faithful theology. This is not to say that God has
left himself without theological witnesses in the history of the
church. And yet, theology is not free in itself, nor do we know of
any divine empowerment of it that would allow us to say that it is
self-authenticating.

How, then, is a liberating theology free? Whenever and
wherever it responds to the reality of God disclosed in Jesus
Christ and the free, liberating word of God in the Bible, theology
itself is liberated and placed in the service of human freedom. Its
freedom is thus a freedom *in* obedience and *for* service. These
forms of freedom, however, are possible for theology only if it is

free *from* other commitments, authorities, and requirements. Therefore we must first consider the need for theology to be free from all other claims that would distract it from its vocation.

A. *Ideological and academic authority*

To begin with, theology finds freedom in obedience to the liberating word of God only if it is free from all other *authority*. It will not go about its task, in the words of Barmen,

> as though the church could and would have to acknowledge as a source of its proclamation, apart from and besides this one Word of God, still other events and powers, figures and truths, as God's revelation.[7]

How can a theology speak a word of liberation and hope against sexual oppression if the deity in whose name it speaks is merely the apotheosis of its own sexual consciousness? How can a theology bring the liberating word of God to a nation enslaved by its own nationalism if it, itself, is nationalistic? National chauvinism is blatant, not only in the more extreme symbols and ceremonies of the Aryan Nation and other representatives of the American religious right, but in all forms of civil religion. The authority of male chauvinism in theology is clearly evident in Catholicism's refusal to admit women into the priesthood and in Protestantism's reluctance to admit women ministers into the parish. Such idolatrous projections of male prejudice upon the divine, however, ought not to be met by counter projections from women — which can only amount to an extension of heteronomous authority over theology. Rabbi Susan Schnur, commenting on Rosemary Radford Ruether's *Women-Church*, observes that the liturgies contained in that work "have to do only with the *political*," and that "politics is often the doctrine for which the liturgy is the vehicle (a dog wagged by its tail)."[8]

Theology is in constant danger of being taken over by political authorities. We noted in chapter 1 that Gordon Kaufman, in the name of a politics of ecology and peace, could demand that theology "be judged in terms of the adequacy with which it is fulfilling the objectives we humans set for it."[9] Similarly, Dorothee Soelle can recommend a "political theology" which "holds open an horizon of interpretation in which politics is understood as the comprehensive and decisive sphere."[10] That such a theology is subject to the authority of particular political visions of human good seems to be implied when she goes on to state that "the verification principle of every theological statement is the praxis that enables for the future" — since practical visions of the future are the business of politics.[11] The trouble with accepting such political authority over theology is that such a procedure can so easily and unconsciously be subverted to other ends. Paul Althaus no doubt believed he was engaged in a liberating political theology when he wrote in favor of the nationalization of the German churches under Hitler.

> People of our day are not concerned about peace with God, but with overcoming political calamity in the broadest sense — the mortal distress of a people, the destruction of the national community, the freedom of the *Volk* for its own life, the fulfillment of its particular mission. If that is the key question of our age, the gospel must be preached to it in terms of its "political" concept.[12]

Theology must learn again that "the political is surely a predicate of theology, but theology is never a predicate of the political."[13] For Barth, it is the political action of God and not human political action that must inform faith. The "kingdom of God is . . . among the kingdoms of the world, but . . . confronts and contradicts and opposes them; the revolution of God [is] proclaimed and accomplished already in the man Jesus. The one whom Jesus calls to himself has to stand firm by the revelation of *this* revolution."[14]

The vision of human freedom and justice available from communism, capitalism, or nationalism has nothing to do with the freedom of God. The liberty promised to the daughters and sons of God is neither a synthesis nor distillation of such authorities, and its freedom is more radical and revolutionary than any freedom they can produce.

Political authority is simply one example of a general *ideological conformity* that threaten the freedom of theology today. Allan Boesak defines ideology as "an idea, or system of ideas . . . used to justify and perpetuate existing structures of injustice."[15] Naturally, a theology that serves the cause of liberation will reject ideology in this sense. There are, however, ideologies (that is, comprehensive philosophical, economic, political, and social ideas that shape the life of a culture) which are not in themselves oppressive, and become so only if granted the status of ultimacy. No science, philosophy, or theology exists without ideological commitments, and any claim to the contrary merely exposes the degree to which the one making the claim is subject to an unrecognized ideological control.

For instance, in the case of theology it has long been clear that beneath fundamentalism's claim of independence from philosophy there lies an unwavering, if not primitive, ideological empiricism which holds the word of God hostage to its own peculiar rules of evidence. Dorothy Nelkin calls attention to such ideological empiricism by noting that creationists view "science as an inductive and descriptive process and poorly comprehend the function of theories and models as useful instruments for prediction."[16] This explains, for instance, why creationists fasten upon gaps in fossil records to argue against an evolutionary system in nature and reject radio-isotope dating because it *assumes* a constant rate of change in uranium.[17] Fundamentalist empiricism may be labeled "ideological" because it refuses to accept the axiom of uniformity upon which modern science is based and places in its stead a mythic conception of divine activity — and it may be labeled "primitive" because it is unaware of having done so.

Similarly, when the Dutch Reformed Church of South Africa promoted apartheid, it was not the Bible or the Reformed doctrine of common grace that influenced their thought so much as a barely concealed ideology of nation and race, which they believed found justification in the thought of Abraham Kuyper.[18] Kuyper asserted that the presence of good in a fallen world could be accounted for only by what he called "common grace" — a doctrine he found in Calvin.[19] This sustaining grace of God finds expression, according to Kuyper, in a plurality of life forms and structures, which must be respected and preserved. Such "pluriformity" creates various "spheres" (such as church, state, family, *Volk*, etc.) that exist directly under the sovereign rule of God. This doctrine stimulated in Kuyper certain "liberal" interests, insofar as labor, science, and art were identified as spheres of grace which have their own special integrity and destiny. On the other hand, Kuyper wrote that "every nation has its special task"[20] and a manifest destiny, "determined and appointed by God, through the hidden counsel of his providence."[21] This doctrine was easily put to the service of an Afrikaner theory of racial and cultural superiority. The Afrikaner nationalist H. G. Stoker wrote: "God willed the diversity of Peoples . . . He might have allowed our People to become bastardized with the native tribes as happened with other Europeans. He did not allow it . . . He has a future task for us, a calling laid away."[22] Because this theology included "the corollary that every other ethnic group should also retain its identity,"[23] it offered a handy crutch for the ideology of apartheid. But only a crutch; it was not the origin. When we recollect that Colonial Americans believed and acted in the same way toward American Indians and African slaves, we need not imagine that Kuyper's theology was responsible for apartheid.

Some degree of ideological commitment cannot be avoided. Fundamental axioms are necessary for our understanding of the world, as are the systems of ideas that cluster around such axioms. Ideology, however, must not be allowed to *control* theological work: Theology cannot serve two masters. To the extent that theological presuppositions are controlled by this or that world view, however benign it may be, theology will miss the liberating power of the freedom of God. A liberating theology is free to begin with God and the word of God, and to let that word speak to and against all the other words and ideas that would define and delimit human hope.

The freedom of theology is also threatened by the rather subtle intrusion of *academic authority*. Since the Enlightenment, theology has found itself more and more in the shadows of academic life. In the nineteenth century some (e.g., Ernst Troeltsch, Rudolf Otto) believed this decline might be arrested by forging strategic alliances with the emerging disciplines of psychology, sociology, and historiography. The result, however, was the gradual replacement of theology in the academy by philosophy, psychology, sociology, and history of religions — a process Claude Welch calls the fate of orthodox theologies "as they retreated steadily before the forces of Enlightenment into the backwaters of intellectual and cultural isolation."[24] This absorbtion was challenged by Karl Barth and other representatives of the "theology of crisis" who reasserted the scientific integrity of theology *as* theology. Barth's claim was simply this: "There is no other possible way for theology to prove its 'scientific nature' than by showing . . . at its task of knowledge [that its] work [is] actually done and determined by its object."[25] While theology has no obligation to conform to any particular definition of "science," it can *be* a science if it does the one thing that all rational inquiry must do — let its thought and investigation be guided by the nature of its subject matter. This means that theology must be about God, God as *God*, as God wills to be known. In other words, if theology is to be *scientific*, it must be done on the basis of the presuppositions and content of faith. Any other basis for theology may clothe it in the robes of other sciences, but cannot make it scientific.

The continuing retreat of contemporary American theology into academic subservience illustrates the failure to understand this point. Glancing over the proceedings of a recent meeting of the American Academy of Religion, one may find over five hundred papers, covering a vast array of interests and disciplines, including postmodernism, women's issues, the academic study of religion, narrative theology, rhetoric and ritual, phenomenology, and Zoroastrianism.[26] A few papers are scheduled for an "Evangelical Theology Group," and there are several given under the title "Christology." Otherwise, the vast majority of the papers read do not treat topics of any major interest to Christian faith or reveal any commitment to it. In its frantic attempt to win a place in the university, theology forfeits any valid claim to be scientific insofar as it does not relate itself to its subject matter in a way that is determined by the reality of God or the disclosure of that reality in Jesus Christ.

B. *Consumerism and coercion*

The trendiness by which theology attempts to satisfy the demands of academic authority is but one example of a consumerism that dictates much of what the church does in its preaching, teaching, and writing. A "crystal cathedral" in California constantly reminds that upbeat, self-serving religion is "what sells."[27] Markets, of course, vary. At one place the theological product may have to reflect the conservative views of *Human Events*, while at another only a liberal *The New Republic* will do. But perhaps the most damaging and pervasive demand of the marketplace is that theology be always original and innovative. Since the "death of God" got on the cover of *Time* magazine in the sixties, there has been this lust for the new, to be on "the cutting edge." Thus, David Tracy, in a chapter contributed to *The Thought of Paul Tillich*, recommends that theology be "post-liberal," "post-romantic," "post-orthodox," "post-existential," "post-modern," and, with remarkable candor, "post-theological."[28] (We can only hope that the intellectual myopia signaled by the popularity of the prefix "post-" has reached *its* final stage in Francis Fukuyama's claim that the decline of communism and the victory of American consumerism inaugurates an epoch which can only be understood as "post-historical.")[29] Along the same line, Thomas Altizer celebrates Mark C. Taylor's deconstructionist a-theology as "a truly new theology,"[30] but according to Joseph Prabhu Taylor's work is merely an extension of the "death of God" movement — the rewarming of a kind of "stew" containing "large doses" of Hegel, some Nietzsche, and a dash of Buddhism, the use of which, Prabhu asserts, "appears like retrieving the bath water after throwing out the baby."[31] The demand for innovation finds theological expression also in worship. A letter from a seminary student at one of the most venerable seminaries in the United States speaks of the difficulty of holding a traditional service where, he writes, "they consecrate apples as communion elements, burn *The Book of Common Prayer*, drop crosses from the ceiling, and chant the name of the goddess — all in the name of worship."[32]

Of course, each generation of theologians must speak in the language and to the concerns of its own day, but in light of the present clamor for originality we may look wistfully (if not exactly with approval) upon the boast reported of Charles Hodge that, during the many years of his predominance there, Princeton Theological Seminary had "never brought forward a single original thought."[33] Originality cannot be the intention of theology, and when it is, the product is usually just warmed-over error.

When innovation does not compel theological work, then sometimes something really new and liberating can happen in theology. Luther protested *against* the innovations of the medieval church and turned back to an older Augustinian tradition where he discovered a theology of Christian freedom fit for his own day.[34] Barth tried to follow Calvin, but was forced to correct him, and in doing so produced a uniquely original doctrine of election — a doctrine that delivered the Reformed faith from the oppression of Calvin's "terrible decree" and made all people equal under an election of grace.[35] We have no reason to believe that any desire for fame led theologians like James Cone, Gustavo Gutiérrez, and Phyllis Trible to produce a liberation theology. Rather, there is every indication that they intended only to bring to bear upon their own contexts of oppression the truth hidden in ancient texts and doctrine.

A liberating theology will not seek a hearing by abandoning its proper object to academic authority or innovative titillation. Neither, we must add, will it give over its freedom to authoritative claims which emanate from the church itself. Such a threat faces Catholic theologians who are subject to the discipline of the Roman magisterium. Hans Küng some years ago lost his status as a teacher of Catholic theology at the University of Tübingen, but retained his position as Professor of Theology. Recently, Charles Curran of the Catholic University of America received similar treatment from the Vatican because of his published positions on contraception and homosexuality. In contrast to Küng's case, however, Curran's dismissal as Professor of Moral Theology has threatened his position on the faculty.[36] From a different direction, doctrinal authoritarianism also confronts theological colleagues at Southeastern Baptist Seminary in North Carolina. In 1987, Baptist conservatives under the leadership of Paige Patterson, President of the Criswell Center for Biblical Studies in Dallas, Texas, achieved a majority on the Southeastern Baptist Seminary's Board of Trustees and made Robert Crowley chairman. The result has been the resignation of the president and dean and the threat of dismissal or other punitive action against faculty members who will not embrace the right-wing politics and religious fundamentalism of the new board.[37]

If a liberated theology obedient to the free word of a free God will not give up its own freedom, it should go without saying that it will not require anyone else to do so. We must not deny theological freedom to others. The foreword to Nancy Hardesty's recent book states that the issue of inclusive language for God is no longer "a matter for debate or an item on the theological agenda."[38] Is that really true, or is it rather that such assertions themselves have a chilling effect upon free theological debate? If we cannot approve of the imposition of a fundamentalist view of scripture upon the students and faculty at Southeastern Baptist

Seminary, we ought not to accept the attempt at other seminaries to impose through administrative policy and sanction language about God that is deemed theologically wrong by others. A liberating theology will try through debate to win agreement, but will never attempt to bind consciences through coercion.

To state the matter another way, a liberating theology is freed from the need to be *defensive*. To be sure, theology must defend essential elements of faith. It must engage in controversy, even polemics, if the reality of God and the liberating power of Christ are to be kept clearly before the church. But while it defends, a liberating theology will not be defensive. The circle it draws will not be one that circumscribes its own narrow interests or tradition. If that happens among fundamentalists and political conservatives, it ought not to happen where theology serves the cause of liberation.

Nor, we must add, will a liberating theology operate behind a wall of narcissistic self-interest. A liberating theology can be as little interested in a "women's church" as in a "men's church." Early in *Women-Church*, Rosemary Radford Ruether asks, "How can [a women's church] affirm a specifically women's journey of liberation without becoming separatist and negating the humanity of males?"[39] Unfortunately, the author makes no serious attempt to answer that question, but instead presents an ecclesiology and a collection of liturgies characterized by narcissism, goddess worship, nature mysticism, and sundry superstitious folderol. This is too bad, because there is much wisdom in various of her liturgies dealing with marriage, divorce, lesbianism, sickness, etc. If all young women could receive the counsel and undertake the reflection called for in a "Puberty Rite for a Young Woman,"[40] teenage pregnancies and other forms of sexual exploitation might be reduced dramatically. Used as a liturgy for worship, however, such a rite can only deepen the rift between the sexes in the church. If only Professor Ruether and her colleagues could demythologize their otherwise helpful sociological and psychological insights, their work would better contribute to a church of women *and* men.[41] A liberating theology is free from contentiousness, contrariness, or obstinacy. Its work cannot be done without controversy, but it will enter the lists of theological debate with equal parts of seriousness and good humor.

Theology needs a sense of humor, and has never been well

served by its absence. Humor in theology occurs quite naturally because it "arises out of the still *partial* presence of [the] kingdom, [and expresses] the undeniable incongruity and disproportion between what we and the world still are and what God's grace in Jesus Christ promises."[42] For all his severity, Calvin occasionally could laugh at himself and his theology. At one place in the *Institutes* he tells a joke borrowed from Augustine (which was perhaps that bishop's single attempt at humor the *City of God*). "When a certain shameless fellow mockingly asked a pious old man what God had done before the creation of the world, the latter aptly countered that he had been building a hell for the curious."[43] At another place Calvin has a chuckle over a jest of the schoolmen, who had to explain that the canonical injunction that "everyone of both sexes (*omnis utriusque sexus*) be confessed once a year," did not "refer only to hermaphrodites."[44] In spite of their differences, Barth got along with Rudolf Bultmann and Paul Tillich because of a shared sense of humor. Describing his last meeting with Tillich, Barth wrote: "I warned him that now might be the time to get himself straight. But he didn't seem to want to do that very much."[45] On the other hand, strain continued to mark the relation between Barth and Emil Brunner which, Barth said, was like that of the elephant and the whale: "Both are God's creatures, but they simply cannot meet."[46] "For Barth," writes Migliore, "humor is grounded in the grace, faithfulness, and promise of God . . . Grace creates 'liberated laughter'."[47]

If today the older generation of theologians must remain open and keep a sense of humor, so ought their younger contemporaries, for there is a danger that a collegiality already strained by ecclesiastical competition and the struggle for academic tenure will collapse altogether in an environment of sullenness and resentment. Today we appear in danger of accepting the highly questionable notion that theology can and should be done out of a sense of personal injury and anger. Of course, a proper prophetic anger and indignation belong to the cause of the oppressed. A righteous anger, however, may be distinguished from its opposite according to whether it is expressed on behalf of another or oneself. In this regard we can only wonder again at the anger and resentment which finds expression in one of Rosemary Radford Ruether's liturgies that includes the lines: "Rapists are the shock troops of patriarchy and wife batterers the army of occupation."[48] A theology responsive to the great goodness and mercy of God cannot nurse resentment; rather, it must seek the solidarity required of the daughters and sons of God called to serve the cause of freedom.

c. *Freedom in obedience for service*

To summarize: theology differs from its source in that it is not free in itself. Theology has no freedom that corresponds to the freedom of God. Its freedom is found in obedient service. But theology cannot exercise this freedom if it conforms to this or that ideology, bows to academic authority, or yields to the consumerism which reigns in the marketplace of ideas. Nor can theology find freedom in obedience to the word and will of God if it succumbs to coercion or itself employs such tactics. On the other hand, if theology can resist these temptations, it may discover its proper freedom in obedience to the liberating word and will of God.

Luther, for instance, liberated theology from the ideological control of Thomism when he rejected the classical realism upon which it was based. He interpreted the biblical concepts of grace and human nature without recourse to Aristotelian categories, and thereby, through his doctrines of justification and vocation, liberated the Christian community from spiritual despair and social stratification. Early in this century Reinhold Niebuhr called for the liberation of theology from the competing ideologies of capitalism and communism and discovered a social theology which inspired a generation to take part in the struggle for justice. Not only was his work decisive for the labor movement, but also, and especially through Martin Luther King, he contributed enormously to the cause of racial equality. The history of Christian thought is filled with examples which remind us that a liberating theology must beware of the influence of *all* ideological assumptions, whether of sex, race, or class struggle.

In our time theology needs especially to declare its independence from a nationalist ideology built upon anti-communism. In spite of the manifest collapse of Marxism-Leninism in the Soviet Union and Eastern Europe, anti-communism continues in America to control political debate, government policy, and to a large extent the concerns of the churches. In the presidential campaign of 1988, Vice-President George Bush shaped his military

and foreign policy statements around the assumptions of the
Cold War while Governor Michael Dukakis, fearing to appear
less hawkish than his opponent, followed suit. Thus the momentous changes in the world's political climate went unnoticed
in America's quadrennial political debate.[49] An illustration of
the religious underpinnings for this remarkable blindness may be
found in the influence of Colonel Robert B. Thieme Jr. upon the
household of vice-presidential candidate Dan Quayle. Colonel
Thieme is a right-wing evangelical preacher who "warns that
the United States is imperiled by creeping socialism . . . [and that]
the welfare system . . . the United Nations and the World Council
of Churches . . . are satanic."[50] Today, as a result of *glasnost*
and *perestroika*, new possibilities for peace and security are
emerging; but Cold War thinking continues to influence Western
policy, as in the Bush administration's recent refusal to grant
"most favored nation" trading status to the Soviet Union. A
theology attentive to the present possibilities for peace, a theology
that can help liberate Western democracies from the oppression
suffered and caused by militant anti-communism, must itself be
free of liberal and conservative orthodoxies identified with the left
and the right.

III. The Courage of Theology

A. *To begin at the beginning*

What has been said so far really amounts to this: a liberated and
liberating theology is granted and will display *courage*. Early in
this century Franz Overbeck wrote: "Theology can no longer be
established through anything but audacity."[51] Barth took up this
challenge, but for him "audacity" did not mean the kind of
theological arrogance displayed by some so-called radical theologians whose precocious formulations are all too safe and profit-
able in today's market. Rather, "audacity" meant the courage to go
"against the stream" of all comfortable theology by returning to the
fundamentals of faith.

> Theological work is distinguished from other kinds of work by
> the fact that anyone who desires to do this work . . . [must]
> every day, in fact, every hour . . . begin anew at the begin-
> ning.[52]

For Barth theology does not merely repeat itself or simply walk in a small circle. Against all insistent advice to the contrary, the theologian must begin again and again with God, with God *as* God, with God who is free in himself and free for us in Jesus Christ and the Holy Spirit.

Liberating theology must have the courage to return again and again to the triune God in whom alone real possibilities for freedom are found. This was what was at stake in the recent John Hick case. A professor of philosophy and theology at Birmingham University and lately at Claremont Graduate School, Hick rejects the doctrine of the Trinity on the grounds that the particularity and ultimacy of its claim prohibit ecumenical understanding and acceptance of other religions, and thus contributes to cultural disharmony and global violence. Furthermore, according to Hick, the benefits of Christ are not dependent upon the dogma of his divinity.[53] For some, Professor Hick's anti-trinitarianism was simply a test of the extent to which the church could be inclusive — whether in an increasingly ecumenical environment it could allow a minister the freedom to teach and preach a unitarian view. Others, however, understood that a much larger issue was involved. In a memorandum prepared at the request of the Presbytery of San Gabriel in 1987, E. David Willis defended the necessity of a trinitarian confession because it

> helps the church keep straight the nature and direction of God's liberating and empowering purposes . . . In the incarnation God is living out an effectively transforming encounter and presence with, in the midst of, as one of, those who need nothing less than the intervention of God's self . . . The liberating reality, of which other experiences of freedom and empowerment are intimations, is the life, ministry, passion, death, resurrection and active presence of our incarnate Lord. It is ultimately only through the servant lordship of this one that we too are freed to share in God's liberating activity in the world.[54]

B. *To accept forgiveness*

The courage to begin again at the beginning, to begin with God the Father, Son, and Holy Spirit, means that a liberating theology must do its work in the light of the forgiveness of sin. Theologians, too, have to accept this forgiveness as their own. They cannot begin with the freedom and liberating power of God if they are preoccupied with their own inadequacy and failure. Such guilt-consciousness can only compel theologians to attach themselves to one or another political philosophy or strategy in a futile attempt to justify themselves. To say that theology must be done in light of the forgiveness of sins is not, however, an appeal to cheap grace, flabby moral consciousness, or a pop-psychology of positive reinforcement — we are not "OK." Theology must recognize, resist, and fight the sin manifest in the powers of oppression. There is already too much reluctance in the church to condemn precisely those political, economic, and social authorities that brutalize and diminish human life. Nor will a theology undertaken in light of the forgiveness of sin fail to recognize its solidarity in sin with those authorities. In this respect we still have much to learn from Reinhold Niebuhr, who reminds us of the degree to which we are "inclined to bow to [the state's] pretensions and to acquiesce in its claims of authority."[55] Nevertheless, a theology of the free and liberating grace of God will know that it, too, stands under that grace. A decision for the justice of God means a decision for the righteousness of God which, as Luther taught supremely, is not our righteousness, but an "alien rightness" that we must accept as our own in faith.[56] If we do not understand that the righteousness of God, which is always on the side of the poor and oppressed, is a righteousness also available to us in faith by grace alone, then the right and justice for which we struggle will not be the justice and righteousness of God. Instead it will merely be an extension of our own self-justifying values. If we do not see God's righteousness as a gift we have been given, we will forfeit the hope that comes from knowing that "God's righteousness triumphs when [humanity] has no means of triumphing."[57]

The cause of liberation is not aided by the guilty conscience of Western theology, however inescapable such guilt may be. From the early church to the present theology has baptized oppressions of all sorts — anti-Semitism, social hierarchy, state brutality, misogyny, racism — the list goes on. But it does not help when theology, overcome by its own guilt, accepts as "right" some other vision and promise for human life than that freely offered in the death and resurrection of Jesus Christ. "The Kairos

Document" from South Africa may represent a case in point. Its framers were preoccupied with the failure of even the best theology to address effectively the violence and tragedy of apartheid. Thus they condemned not only the "state theology" of the racist Afrikaner denominations, but as well the "church theology" of reconciliation represented, among others, by Beyers Naudé, Desmond Tutu, and Alan Boesak—all courageous participants in the liberation struggle. The day may come when the church must take its place on the barricades with the oppressed majority of South Africa — and who could blame those actually suffering under state terror if they believe that day has arrived? But by rejecting specifically the church's call for reconciliation in favor of a revolutionary call for action, the authors of "The Kairos Document" risk the reproduction of oppression in revolutionary violence and miss the transforming and liberating power of the forgiveness of sins.[58]

A liberating theology will have the courage, even the audacity, to claim for itself the free grace of a free God. It will confess its culpability and sin. It will not gloss over its past and present failures, but it will in faith claim for itself the righteousness of God which it proclaims on behalf of the oppressed. It will confess the forgiveness of sins — from which there follows, writes Barth,

> a political attitude, decisively determined by the fact that man is made responsible to all those who are poor and wretched in [God's] eyes, [and] summoned on his part to espouse the cause of those who suffer wrong. Why? Because in them it is manifest to him what he himself is in the sight of God; because the living, gracious, merciful action of God towards him consists in the fact that God himself in his own righteousness procures right for *him*, the poor and wretched; because he and all men stand in the presence of God as those for whom right can be procured only by God himself. The man who lives by the faith [of the forgiveness of sins] stands under a political responsibility . . . As surely as he himself lives by the grace of God he cannot evade this claim. He cannot avoid the question of human rights. He can only will and affirm a state which is based on justice. By any other political attitude he rejects the divine justification.[59]

A liberating theology responsive to the freedom of God, a freedom which acts in love, liberating men and women from oppression, will exhibit the courage of faith — a faith which rejects all other authority and any other righteousness and justice than that which God alone empowers and inspires. For some, that kind of courage asks a great price. We have our own book of martyrs — Dietrich Bonhoeffer, Steven Biko, Bishop Oscar Romero, Martin Luther King. For most of us, however, there is demanded a much smaller courage — the courage to relinquish a preoccupation with guilt (behind which lurks a pride of self) and accept the great freedom that God has given us as theologians to make God's cause of human liberation our own.

In the next chapter we must ask what the freedom of God means for the goal of liberation, for the shape and character of human freedom itself.

6

Revolutionary Freedom

Introduction

Our theme has been "the freedom of God and human liberation."
By "liberation" we do not mean only an idea or general principle.
The word does not point to some far-off utopia, but to a
possibility for life *now* that serves justice, peace, and wholeness.
In short, "liberation" implies human freedom.

What people understand by "freedom" is at once multifarious
and problematic. For some, freedom means to live without *con-
straint*; for others, without *restraint*; for some, it means the right
to give full expression to one's powers; for others, it means the
unimpeded right to impose one's power upon others. For Hegel
and Marx, freedom meant the conformity of life to the processes
of life and history; for Nietzsche, it meant the actualized will to
challenge any such process. For Tillich, freedom meant the
overcoming of authority; for the apostle Paul, it meant being a
slave of Christ. If we are not to get lost in such a labyrinth, we
must keep in mind our general principle and examine the nature
of human freedom in its relation to the freedom of God. We have
seen that the freedom of God is not a mere theological abstraction, but is the way in which God exists — a way which has a
definite structure and meaning. God is free *in* himself, *from* other
being, *for* us in Jesus Christ, but also free *from* his ways of being *for*
us. We found that this structure has meaning for our understanding of the way God's freedom empowers and directs the cause of
human liberation. The same will hold true for our understanding
of human freedom.

In any examination of human freedom in relation to the
freedom of God, it is important not to misconstrue that relationship. In the previous chapter we discussed the way the Bible as

witness bears a "correspondence" to the freedom of God. We could not say the same of even the best theology, because although it too is a human word about God, we do not have the witness of the church that theology is taken up and used by God in the same way as the Bible. When the issue is human freedom, however, this scruple becomes an absolute prohibition.

If in theology we find no predictable correspondence to divine freedom, in what is usually meant by human "freedom" we find a *contradiction* masquerading as a correspondence. We want to believe that our freedom corresponds to divine freedom. We want to be free *in* ourselves, "autonomous," a law to ourselves in a way which apes the aseity of God. We seek a promethean grandeur that frees the self *from* this or that undesirable influence. The self thus secured can then assert its freedom *for* the enjoyment of natural rights or special privilege according to its tastes. And since our tastes and inclinations contradict each other (as need for love conflicts with a desire for independence, or an unrestrained life style with a desire for health), we display in tragic irony our own way of being free *from* our freedom *for*. Insofar as human freedom is understood as autonomy, we must say that there exists only a negative correspondence between our freedom and the freedom of God. If in what follows we will have to speak of a positive correlation between God's freedom and ours, that will be said only of the freedom that God creates in us — a freedom we are given and given ever anew so that it can never be something we can have on our own.

I. The Failure of Autonomy

A. *The ambiguity of revolution*

We cannot deny the validity of revolutionary struggle. When oppression takes root in social, economic, and political structures, then movements for liberation must become revolutionary and seek to turn society away from injustice and toward a better vision of the human future. For this reason the hand of God can often be seen in political revolution. But when revolution serves merely to give political shape to human autonomy, it must inevitably conflict with the freedom of God. As Reinhold Niebuhr, Karl Barth, Paul Tillich, and more lately Paul Lehmann, have reminded us, a profound ambiguity accompanies all revolutions.[1] In pushing forward toward justice, revolutions tend also to revolve back to the oppressive tactics of the regimes they supplant. Illustrations abound. The French Revolution soon enough returned to monarchial, even imperial, rule. The Russian Revolution, according to Niebuhr, illustrated this reversion in a pious "messianism" in which "every weapon became morally permissible."[2] Not every revolution is as brutal as Stalin's return to Czarist terror, certainly not the Cuban, and even less the Nicaraguan, but Uganda comes to mind, as does the forgotten holocaust in Cambodia.

We need not look so far afield to see the ambiguity of revolution. The American Revolution was the first successful turn from monarchial toward republican government and is rightly celebrated on that account. On the other hand, if in that revolution there was no reign of terror, the Tories who fled to Ontario and Nova Scotia experienced a popular brutality of which American history cannot be proud. Nor can we forget the systematic violence which European Americans inflicted upon American Indians before, during, and after the revolution. The United States Constitution established a new vision of human rights, but it also reinforced inherited structures of privilege and power in respect to property and the servitude of women and blacks. Moreover, for all its amendments and social progress, that document, with its "Bill of Rights," has not established meaningful freedom for all. In her American journal, *Alone Together*, the Russian writer Elena Bonner describes a conversation with a bearded "beach bum" in Miami. "We spoke of his country and mine, what was good and what was bad. I said, 'We don't have freedom.' He said, 'We do -- to jump in the ocean.' "[3] The American Revolution has not made good on its promise of freedom for others. Consumed with our own national autonomy, we blunder about the world serving oppressions our revolution intended to remove. Again, Bonner notes about her American friends: ". . . they sleep peacefully. They do not notice that they have deprived and ruined the sleep of millions of other people."[4]

Now all of this does not mean that we should reject revolution or even revolutionary violence as a possible way of obedience to the liberating will of God. If we are unwilling to repudiate the violence which attended the French and American Revolutions, we obviously cannot deny its necessity elsewhere. Barth could even maintain that "revolution is the 'minister of God,'"[5] but we must understand the problem, which is, as Barth wrote in his *Romans*, that

> even the most radical revolution can do no more than set what exists against what exists ... in itself [it is] simply a justification and confirmation of what already exists.[6]

Under the conditions of finitude we cannot escape what Niebuhr called the tragic "ironies of history" produced by the inexorable laws of nature and history operating within the closed circle of human pride. If the struggle for freedom is to succeed, it must have recourse to another possibility — which is what Barth had in mind when he wrote "the 'revolutionary' [must] sacrifice his 'revolutionary action' to 'the action of God.'"[7] That is the real and only hope for revolutionary praxis, and that is why Paul Lehmann insists upon a political "transfiguration" in which "revelation and revolution" can be brought together in a way that "bears and exposes the secret and the power by which revolutions are preserved from their fate, which is to devour themselves."[8]

B. *The nature of autonomy*

If the structural transformation of revolutionary justice can occur, in Moltmann's words, "only when previously unexpected possibilities are at hand,"[9] our understanding of freedom must itself undergo a radical, revolutionary change.

The word "freedom," like "love," has been so distorted and trivialized in our culture as to defy serious definition. Let us begin, however, by setting aside those common uses that refer only to civil rights and privileges or to a life of self-fulfillment, and considering a claim concerning the meaning of freedom in its most basic form — a claim presented in Dostoevsky's familiar story of *The Grand Inquisitor*. The setting is Seville during the Inquisition. Jesus appears in the streets and is recognized by all. He raises a child from the dead. The Cardinal Inquisitor, who also recognizes him, enters the adoring throng and without hesitation has Jesus seized. The crowd meekly submits. The Cardinal visits Jesus' cell that night and a one-way conversation begins with the question:

"Is it you? . . . why have you come to hinder us? . . . Did you not say 'I will make you free?' But now you have seen these 'free' men . . . At last we have completed that work in your name. For fifteen centuries we have been wrestling with your freedom, but now it is ended and over for good . . . Today, people are more persuaded than ever that they are completely free, yet they have brought their freedom to us and laid it humbly at our feet . . . Was this what you did? Was this your freedom? . . . Man was created a rebel; and how can rebels be happy? . . . I tell you that man is tormented by no greater anxiety than to find someone to whom he can hand over quickly that gift of freedom with which the unhappy creature is born . . . Did you forget that man prefers peace and even death to freedom of choice in the knowledge of good and evil? . . . Instead of taking possession of man's freedom, you increased it . . . and burdened mankind forever with its sufferings."[10]

For Dostoevsky the Grand Inquisitor represents the totalitarian state and the church. These powers offer what Jesus refused in his temptations, namely, bread and authority. Such gifts make women and men who are "weak and vile" happy, and says the Cardinal, "only we, we who guard the mystery will be unhappy."[11] He ends his speech with the declaration that he will burn Jesus, but Jesus never says a word. Dostoevsky concludes:

The old man longed for him to say something, however bitter and terrible. But he suddenly approaches the old man in silence and softly kisses him on his bloodless aged lips. That was his whole answer. The old man shudders . . . He goes to the door, opens it, and says to him: "Go and come no more . . . Come not at all, never, never!"[12]

This story of unparalleled dramatic insight says much about human freedom. Dostoevsky understands that there is a freedom for which Christ came to make us free. He also sees that human beings are quick to deliver the burden of personal liberty over to authority, and in so doing make themselves weak and vile. They do not want real freedom, but in their self-inflicted misery believe themselves free. The truth of Dostoevsky's observation is all around us. We in the Western democracies view with disapproval the inclination of some in Eastern Europe and the Soviet

Union to refuse the risks of a free economy in favor of the cheap bread offered by communism, but we fail to notice the way we also sacrifice our freedoms to media-managed elections and the "cheap bread" of deficit spending. All of this is foreseen in Dostoevsky's story, and we cannot appreciate too much the power of his protest against every political and religious utopianism or the courage of his own Christian humanism.

Yet in this drama we encounter a depth of despair that betrays its fundamental understanding of freedom. The problem is that Dostoevsky views freedom as a natural endowment of autonomy. For him freedom is represented by moral choice, which he believes has its model in Jesus' resistance to temptation. Such freedom is not so much a divine gift as a gift of divinity because, according to the serpent's testimony in Gen. 3:5, to know good from evil means to "be like God." This autonomous freedom places a terrible burden upon humanity. For Dostoevsky, it is at once the grandeur and the tragedy of human life. Autonomous freedom confronts us with the Herculean obligation to be and to live on our own. That we do not do so the author considers a universal and unavoidable (if at the same time inexplicable) tragedy. Thus, according to Dostoevsky, freedom, defined by the way we actually live it, is no "gift" at all, but a curse — and a "weak and vile" humanity can hardly be blamed for wanting to get rid of it.

c. *The self-contradiction of autonomy*

What shall we say about this autonomous freedom with which, according to Dostoevsky, we are naturally endowed? We believe that we have this freedom in the form of freedom of choice, although there are many reasons to doubt it. The more we learn about physics, the more we may wonder whether and to what extent some unified field theory, involving perhaps five or six dimensions we know nothing about, prove us to be literally "on a string" — as Princeton's Professor Witten has proposed.[13] We may wonder whether and to what extent genetic and environmental conditioning controls our thoughts and actions. Deterministic theories are by nature irrefutable. Voltaire said that the only thing to be done with a determinist is to beat him until he admits his tormentor is free to stop. Perhaps he was right, for even if we cannot refute determinism, we will not deny our freedom of thought and will. We know we are free to choose, but what good is it finally if we can choose only from among the possibilities within the closed and sometimes vicious circle of our own existence? If freedom is only autonomy, will not such "self-rule" sooner or later choose evil over good, or authority over liberty? Will not such a choice be a *function* of autonomous freedom rather than, as Dostoevsky asserted, a denial of it? Why else should the masses think they are happy unless the totalitarianism to which they have freely submitted is a logical extension of their own self-will, indeed, its fullest and final expression?

I think we must replace Dostoevsky's assessment of autonomous freedom with one that better explains his story. Autonomy under the conditions of existence is self-bondage, and real freedom, as Ricoeur has put it, is "deliverance from self-enslavement."[14] Autonomy is not a real freedom which we somehow inexplicably forfeit, but is at its root a self-enslavement which must find expression in other forms of enslavement. By applying a little Derridian analysis to *The Grand Inquisitor*, we may discover certain elements that agree with this assessment of autonomy in contradiction to Dostoevsky's main thesis. The polarity the Cardinal assumes between autonomy and slavery is unwittingly inverted when he observes that while the enslaved are "happy" in their miserable condition, only the privileged "who guard the mystery will be unhappy." This inversion shows that, if freedom is only the exercise of autonomy, the distinction between master and slave is a difference that makes no difference.

Such freedom cannot be identified with the freedom of God, the freedom for which Christ made us free. The Grand Inquisitor thought that Jesus' refusal to cast himself down from the temple was a supreme act of moral choice. But was it? "You knew," the Cardinal said, "that you would be tempting God . . . and would have been dashed to pieces against the earth which you had come to save."[15] Can we believe that such a denial of his vocation presented itself to Jesus as a real option? Were not all of the temptations answered in his response to the first, "You shall worship the Lord God and him only shall you serve" (Luke 4:8)? The freedom of the Son of God was not disclosed in a courageous, personal choice among alternatives, but in his decision to let his life be determined by his vocation, to *be* what he was, the Son of God, obedient to the Father.

What then of our freedom under God? Dostoevsky intends to present freedom as heroic autonomy, but at the very end of the story a contradiction of this view takes place that may easily be overlooked. Jesus once more stands condemned by an authority no more happy with its lot than Pontius Pilate. Against such autonomy Jesus remains stubbornly silent. He will not become one more item to be calculated or chosen by such "discriminating" freedom. The Inquisitor, bound by the same autonomous freedom as his oppressed subjects, can only continue to make the same decision that authority has always made about Jesus — to kill him. Jesus, however, as befits the bearer of divine freedom, acts in love. He "suddenly approaches" the old man and kisses him — and the Cardinal opens the door. The Cardinal's act of liberation, an act brought about by the divine decision of love, an act compelled by the divine mercy, an act contradictory to the decision and will of the Inquisitor's autonomous authority, that act is (apart from the actions of Christ) the only free act in the story. The Grand Inquisitor acted freely because he acted in obedience, if only momentarily and fleetingly, to the liberating power and love of Christ.

The Inquisitor was wrong. Freedom is not autonomy. It is not being left alone with our own self-governance. "Who," asks Barth, "can exercise a worse tyranny over us than the god in our own breast" — the god who is merely a projection of ourselves?[16] Eberhard Busch reports that toward the end of his life Barth was troubled by a dream. He saw an immense and cold desert and one person sitting alone. "Does that trouble you?" a voice asked.[17] What can be worse, more hellish, than to be left alone with our own "freedom"? But if this is the case, how can we not be thankful that God has not and will not leave us alone in our autonomy, but out of his own sovereign freedom offers us real freedom?

Freedom under God does not impose a divine determinism which removes all spontaneity, responsibility, and decision from life. To the contrary, it provides the only possibility for real freedom. The freedom of God *from* the finite categories of cause and effect allows God to break through the closed circle of our autonomous self-enslavement and make us free. That in doing so God grants us space and time for the exercise of responsibility and choice is clear. It is also clear that we are called by God to make sure that others are not deprived of their freedom. The responsibility to which we are called, however, is not a matter of selection among many possibilities and even less an invitation to exercise an autonomous discretion over them. We are not faced with a variety of options. Only one way is open. We are invited to follow it, and we are free to do so. We are not free to do otherwise. We may do so, but neither that decision nor its result may be called freedom. It is only another expression of self-bondage. "Freedom," wrote Barth, "means being in a spontaneous and therefore willing agreement with the sovereign freedom of God."[18]

If revolutions fail to achieve liberation, if they merely reduplicate past oppression, if autonomy leads merely to self-enslavement, then the task of theology is to bring to the cause of human liberation the new and unexpected possibilities of the radical and revolutionary freedom of God.

II. God's Revolution

In the mystery and majesty of aseity, God is God — absolutely, uniquely free. We must therefore expect, in God's freedom for us, the absolutely new and unprecedented.

> Behold, I am doing a new thing; now it springs forth, do you not perceive it? I will make a way in the wilderness and rivers in the desert. (Isa. 43:18)

If the church does not expect the new, if it believes that the liberating will of God must operate according to the laws of nature, the precedents of history, or according to this or that ideology or system of values, then it can only chose among the most promising of revolutionary theories. If this is all it can do, then it can only "set what exists against what already exists" and thereby add to the ambiguity of revolutionary effort.[19]

The failure of theology to expect the unexpected from God has rendered Christian faith marginal in liberation praxis. Neglect of this principle may well account for the failure of the German Reformation to respond correctly to the Peasants' Revolt of 1525. Luther seems to have had a narrowly defined liberation agenda shaped by perceptions of the interests of the lesser nobility as well as the rights of the rising bourgeoisie to whom he belonged.[20] He was therefore unable to see the hand of God in the Peasants' Revolt and reacted violently against it. The feasibility of success for such a revolution was still centuries away, but the failure of the church to see in that uprising a new possibility for human freedom caused at the outset an alienation between Protestantism and the working classes which continues into our own day.

In the nineteenth century the same failure to imagine a radically new social meaning of the gospel can be seen in the Ritschlians, who tended to associate the social value of God with the established norms of their own society. When in the 1920s Immanuel Hirsch approved of national socialism, even identifying its revivification of German nationalism and racism with the will of God, he was only repeating the same error.[21] Right-wing American theology interprets the meaning of the freedom of God according to the imperatives of middle class democratic theory and its aggressive exportation of American values. Thus it contributed to the Cold War, and to all the violence and tragedy that followed.

In our time theologies of liberation have broken away from middle class definitions of freedom and have taken up the cause of liberation from the perspective of the impoverished and oppressed themselves. In the voices of black Americans and black South Africans, Latin Americans and women, the speech of theology now bears the inflection of the experience of injustice. We must be grateful for these voices, but the question and danger still remain. If the struggle for liberation is to avoid the failures and errors of the past, we cannot be reminded too often that God stands on the side of the oppressed always in new and unexpected ways. God will not necessarily follow our agendas — shaped as they may be by Western democratic theory, Marxist analysis, revolutionary praxis, or racial or sexual self-perception.

God's revolutionary "new thing" comes into view wherever revolutionary effort is saved from the self-destructive circle of autonomy. There are times (which Tillich called moments of *kairos*) when the reality of God touches and turns the course of history back to his own purposes. The early seventies may have witnessed such a *kairos*, for if the freedom of God was not at work then, how did it happen that a powerful nation at war in Vietnam allowed its guns to be stopped by the flowers of children? If the politics of God is not able to transform the laws of self-interest and racial pride, on what basis could we even pray for peace and justice in South Africa? If the advantages of a free market economy now serve to revolutionize a stagnant and oppressive socialism in China and the Soviet Union, what will rescue those societies from the spiritual stultification and selfishness that appears endemic in Western industrial democracies? We must expect the unexpected.

The revolutionary politics of God does not revolve within the hopeless circle of human autonomy, but breaks out to find new possibilities for justice and peace. When revolutionary struggle allows the freedom of God to inform its theory and practice, then there occurs, writes Paul Lehmann, a

> transfiguration . . . the happening according to which the providential-eschatological pressure . . . upon human affairs gives political shape to a divinely appointed new and freeing and fulfilling human order . . . [This] transfiguration is the unveiling of the hidden destiny of revolution in the miraculous inversion of its dynamics from self-justifying self-destruction to the concrete practice of an order whose presupposition and condition is freedom.[22]

III. Revolutionary Freedom

A. *The gift of freedom*

What does the revolutionary freedom of God mean for individual, personal freedom? In the first place, because it is *God's* freedom which empowers and sustains human freedom, it must be recognized as absolutely prior to our freedom. This claim constitutes the whole thrust of our project. Because God is free in himself and from other being so that he can be free for us in Jesus Christ, we have to acknowledge right from the start that freedom is something that belongs to God before it belongs to us. Freedom is a divine activity and work before it becomes ours. God *makes* us free.

This means that freedom is a gift. "Human freedom," writes Barth, "is the gift of God in the free outpouring of his grace. To call a man free is to recognize that God has given him freedom."[23] And if it is a gift, it cannot be a claim. We may claim freedom for others — in fact, we must see to it that others are not victimized by the limitless claims of other autonomies, whether national, economic, racial, or sexual. We must also protect our own civil and social liberty; but it can never be a sign of the presence of the freedom of God when we clamor for a maximization of our own freedom. The insistence that personal behavior be given unlimited scope can only be an expression of the desire to return to the self-created bondage of autonomy. The freedom of God, real freedom, is already there for us. It is a gift.

The freedom of God is always a "new thing." Freedom, then, means giving up the old, worn-out compulsions that accompany autonomy. We want freedom from our labor, freedom from so much responsibility, freedom from old marriages and commitments, freedom from authority, freedom from having to exercise authority. In fact, as Dostoevsky makes clear, we even want freedom from having to choose and decide. The autonomous self wants finally to be free of its own poor freedom. The freedom of God, however, is revolutionary precisely in the fact that it will not provide that kind of "bread" — the bread of dependence offered by the Grand Inquisitor. The freedom of God means an *in*dependence from what before preoccupied and oppressed. In the first edition of his *Romans*, Barth wrote, "What Christ brings is in fact the revolution, the dissolution of all dependence." But then he added, "the [new] dependence which Christ gives us is actually the freedom of God."[24] Under the power and grace of that dependence, all other of life's burdens and obligations can be met in freedom.

B. *Freedom in obedience*

Revolutionary freedom is therefore freedom in obedience. The Grand Inquisitor was wrong about Jesus. He thought that Jesus had made no claim upon humanity but only left it with the awful burden of autonomy. The claim of Christ, however, was at once more absolute in its authority and more radical in its freedom than the Inquisitor understood. His claim was no less than that of the creator over the creature, and it involved a lordship and authority which overcame the world and all of its powers and principalities. With this sovereignty there came a command, the command to believe the gospel of liberation and live as those who, according to Gal. 5:1, have been freed "for freedom." There are those in the church today who, because of the excesses of patriarchy, reject all claims of authority and even demand that we drop the "lordship" of Christ from our theological and liturgical vocabularies. Upon the same analysis, process theology claims that the exercise of divine authority can best be understood as "persuasion." These proposals cannot be welcomed, for they cannot achieve liberation: they can only throw us back again into the bondage of competing autonomies. Only in obedience to Christ the Lord can true freedom be found.

Freedom in obedience is radical freedom, because the obedience required is not to law, but to grace. Faith owes obedience, not to some abstract absolute, but to the God who acts, lives, and loves in freedom. Thus the command that we must obey establishes our freedom, because it demands that we accept this grace as our own, that we understand ourselves as women and men who have been justified, whose sins have been borne and borne away by Christ, and who thus may live in freedom. The gospel invites us to a freedom more radical than any envisioned in revolutionary theory, because it is a freedom that must be lived out in terms of grace and not the law of personal or collective autonomy.

"For freedom Christ has set us free, stand fast therefore, and do not submit again to a yoke of slavery" (Gal. 5:1). That is good news. But freedom under God may well strike us with awe and dread, for it denies us every authority except the grace of Christ. For instance, in respect to the moral life, we are denied the autonomous discrimination which undergirds prudential ethics. Dietrich Bonhoeffer makes the point in his *Ethics* that Jesus never answered questions about moral behavior directly, because he refused to let the freedom he brought to be drawn again into the "human either/or."[25] The freedom of Christ cannot be confused with the choices that preoccupy autonomy. For Bonhoeffer, it could only mean living under grace in the world with fear and trembling. This kind of freedom involves, to use a term introduced earlier, a "metacritical reflexivity" in which we act in the knowledge that in Christ (1) we are liberated from our own and the world's autonomy, and therefore, (2) we are directed to responsible decisions under the conditions of sinful existence. Then, however, by an "after thinking," (3) we are required to acknowledge that even our best judgment will not in any case conform to the will of God. That is the movement Dietrich Bonhoeffer made when he aided the attempt on Hitler's life and did not disavow the guilt he thereby acquired. That is why his imprisonment and death can be rightly viewed as a glorious example of Christian freedom. The radicality of freedom under God consists in our being directed to submit to law (although we have been saved from law), to live with guilt (although we are justified), and to act by the direction of our own judgment (although that is not our freedom). We can do so, because the freedom of God is a gift ever given, a grace ever offered. In the light of that gift we can and must, in a sense, live on our own.

Freedom in obedience means living in faith under the limited conditions of our humanity. We are not, however, left without a general rule for the exercise of freedom. As the meaning of God's freedom in himself and from other being is known to us only because God is free *for us*, so too the revolutionary freedom of the children of God is discovered only insofar as it is a freedom *for others*. The freedom of Christ that sets us free was first recognized as a freedom that preached "good news to the poor," "release to the captives," and "liberty [for] those who are oppressed." Christ was the freedom of God for us; his freedom consisted in the fact that he was "a man for others." That freedom under God is a freedom for others is obviously not understood by oppressors, who are in bondage to their own autonomous authority. Nor is it easy for those who suffer oppression to see this "other-directed" quality of freedom. If, however, this condition of freedom is not also understood and practiced even among the oppressed, then revolution can only collapse again into autonomy. Perhaps this is why Letty Russell once insisted that, "For Christian women the experience of new freedom leads to responsibility . . . [and] brings with it a commission to act in ministry and service to the world with which they groan."[26]

Christian freedom is not autonomy (self-law/rule). It is freedom under the governance of God's grace. Tillich spoke of "theonomy" (God's law/rule) as a condition for freedom, because he thought that under God personal autonomy could be restored to a positive use. Heteronomy ("other" law/rule), he believed, could only diminish and violate human life. We have seen, however, that all those other (heternomous) authorities and powers which oppress human life are but the ultimate expressions of what our own autonomy asserts. The only real possibility for human freedom is found in God. Therefore, because our freedom comes from God who is "other," because it is a freedom "other" than our own and can find expression only in service to "an other," because it is so ruled by "otherness," we can speak of Christian freedom as "heteronomous freedom," that is, freedom as the "law of the other."[27]

Finally, freedom undertaken in obedience is *joy*. The freedom of God is more revolutionary than the freedom of our revolutions, for God's freedom alone breaks out of the closed circle of autonomy. In the freedom of God "the creation itself will be set free from its bondage to decay and obtain the glorious liberty of the children of God" (Rom. 8:21). For this reason the freedom we have from God is joy.

> Freedom is a great gift, totally unmerited and wondrous beyond understanding, It awakens the receiver to true selfhood and new life, It is a gift from *God*, from the source of all goodness, an ever-new token of his faithfulness and mercy. [This] gift is unambiguous and cannot fail. Through this gift [we] who [were] irretrievably separated and alienated from God [are] called into discipleship. This is why freedom is joy . . . We may . . . presently know and enjoy this freedom through the abiding Spirit of the Father and the Son . . . God's gift is there for all. It is poured out at the beginning of our journey, at its destination, and most certainly also in our present plight. Freedom is waiting here and now to be received and lived out in joy.[28]

If we are to live out the freedom that God has for us in Jesus Christ, we must not confuse our own images of freedom with God's freedom. We must learn to think metacritically of the way that God is free in himself and from all other being, for only such a God as that can overcome the tragic inevitabilities of human history and really "set the prisoners free." We must learn to read the free and liberating word of God without imposing upon it messages of our own contrivance, and we must liberate theology from every principality and power which would keep it from effectively articulating the liberating power of God. Only as we learn that true freedom is to be found in obedient service to God and our neighbor will we discover the "glorious liberty" that belongs to the children of God.

NOTES

1. Recovering the Freedom of God

1. Unless otherwise noted biblical quotations are taken from the Revised Standard Version.

2. Karl Barth, *Church Dogmatics*, vol. 2/1 (Edinburgh: T. & T. Clark, 1956), 386. Hereafter *CD*, vol., part., page   .

3. Daniel L. Migliore, *Called to Freedom: Liberation Theology and the Future of Christian Doctrine* (Philadelphia: Westminster Press, 1980), 15ff.

4. Exodus 34:6–7.

5. John Calvin, *Institutes of the Christian Religion*, ed. John T. McNeill (Philadelphia: Westminster Press, 1960), bk. 1, chap. 10, par. 2. Hereafter *Institutes*, bk.. chap.. par.

6. *CD* 2.2.54.

7. This other-directedness of Jesus was emphasized in Paul Tillich's Christology. Cf. Paul Tillich, *Systematic Theology*, vol. 2 (Chicago: University of Chicago Press, 1957), 126.

8. "I'm going to get my rightful place. I'm going to rule and I'm going to reign." *Spartanburg Herald Journal* (June 27, 1987), from an Associated Press article by Gil Broyler.

9. Carol P. Christ and Judith Plaskow, ed. *Womanspirit Rising: A Feminist Reader in Religion*. (San Francisco: Harper & Row, 1979), 147. In this respect the actress and New Age writer, Shirley MacLaine, appears at least more democratic when she claims that, "If you don't see me as God, its because you don't see yourself as God." *Time* (Dec. 7, 1987). 72.

10. In Japan, where theological interest in feminism or the civil rights of Koreans has been slow to develop, a liberation theology has taken up the cause of the "*eta*" or "*burakumin*," an oppressed class of workers traditionally associated with the despised trades of butchering and tanning.

11. Eberhard Jüngel, *Karl Barth: A Theological Legacy* (Philadelphia: Westminster Press, 1986), 95.

12. Cf. Reinhold Seeberg, *Textbook of the History of Doctrines*, vol. 1 (Grand Rapids, Baker Book House, 1964) 290; and Paul Tillich, *Systematic Theology*, vol. 1., 235ff.

13. Paul Tillich, *Systematic Theology*, vol. 2, 12.

14. Seeberg, *History of Doctrines*, bk. 1, 292.

15. Tillich, *Systematic Theology*, vol. 1, 245ff.

16. Ludwig Feuerbach, *The Essence of Christianity* (New York: Harper & Row, 1957), 44 and 23. In agreement with Feuerbach, Karl Barth wrote: "We assign to [God] the highest place in our world: and in so doing place him

fundamentally on one line with our selves and with things . . . what is called 'God' is in fact Man." Karl Barth, *The Epistle to the Romans* (London: Oxford University Press, 1953), 44. See also *CD* 2.1.67ff.

17. Nicholas of Cusa, *On Learned Ignorance*, trans. and ed. Jasper Hopkins (Minneapolis: The Arthur J. Banning Press, 1981). In bk. 2, chap. 2, 50–51, Nicholas explains the knowledge to be gained by "not knowing."

18. Friedrich Schleiermacher, *The Christian Faith*, vol. 1., ed. H. R. Mackintosh (New York: Harper & Row, 1963), 131.

19. James C. Livingston, *Modern Christian Thought* (New York: Macmillan Co., 1971), 110.

20. Immanuel Kant, *Critique of Practical Reason*, trans. Lewis White Beck (Indianapolis: The Bobbs-Merrill Co., 1958), 130.

21. Livingston, *Modern Christian Thought*, 155.

22. G. W. F. Hegel, *Lectures on the Philosophy of Religion*, vol. 3, trans. E. B. Speirs and J. B. Sanderson (Atlantic Highlands, N. J.: Humanities Press, Int'l, 1968). Cf. "The Encyclopedia," par. 564.

23. Karl Barth, *Protestant Thought from Rousseau to Ritschl* (New York: Harper and Brothers, 1959), 362; Albrecht Ritschl, *The Christian Doctrine of Justification and Reconciliation*, ed. H. R. Mackintosh (Edinburgh: T. & T. Clark, 1900), 212.

24. *Luther's Works*, vol. 32, ed. George W. Forell (Philadelphia: Muhlenberg Press, 1958), 224.

25. Cf. Roland H. Bainton, *Here I Stand: A Life of Martin Luther* (Nashville: Abingdon Press, 1978), 353ff.

26. One may, however, have to judge as overly familiar the Presbyterian evangelical beach party widely advertized as "fun in the Son." Cf. *The Open Letter* 20 (May/June 1989): 6.

27. Hugh T. Kerr, ed., *A Compend of Luther's Theology* (Philadelphia: Westminster Press, 1943), 27.

28. Quoted in Paul Althaus, *The Theology of Martin Luther* (Philadelphia: Fortress Press, 1966), 225. (Ref. *WA* 37.46).

29. Bainton, *Here I Stand*, 178.

30. Gordon D. Kaufmann, *Theology for a Nuclear Age* (Philadelphia: Westminster Press, 1985).

31. Kaufmann, *Theology*, 19. For Kaufman, theology is also "essentially an activity of imaginative construction" (p. 26). Theology is certainly that, but if it is "essentially" that, on what grounds can theology be distinguished from fiction?

32. Frederick Herzog, *Justice Church* (Maryknoll: Orbis Books, 1980), 90.

33. It is not only the Moral Majority whose theology is shaped in this way. As reported in *The Open Letter* (Sept/Oct 1987), a number of American Presbyterians overtured their General Assembly to turn away various "peace making" proposals placed before that body.

34. Allan Boesak, *Farewell to Innocence* (Maryknoll: Orbis Books, 1977), 14.

35. Tillich, *Systematic Theology*, vol. 1, 245.

36. Even in the Lord's Prayer, "Our Father . . ." is an address permitted only because of the prior fact of the unique sonship of Jesus. Thus Calvin, when introducing his study of the Lord's Prayer, states that "in calling God

'Father,' we put forward the name 'Christ.' With what confidence would anyone address God as 'Father?' Who would break forth into such rashness as to claim for himself the honor of a son [or daughter] of God unless we had been adopted as children of grace in Christ?" *Institutues* 3.20.36.

37. Eberhard Busch, "God is God: The Meaning of a Controversial Formula and the Fundamental Problem of Speaking About God," *The Princeton Seminary Bulletin* 7 (1986): 101–13.

38. Busch, "God is God," 107.

39. Tillich, *Systematic Theology*, vol. 1, 239. Here Tillich defends his use of the *analogia entis*, which links God's being and human being.

40. In what follows we will be guided by the general outline of Barth's discussion of these two points in *CD* 2.1.257ff., and add some supporting evidence of our own.

41. Cf. Bernard W. Anderson, *Understanding the Old Testament* (Englewood Cliffs: Prentice-Hall, 1957), 33ff., and Gerhard Von Rad, *Old Testament Theology* (Edinburgh: Oliver and Boyd, 1962), 180–81.

42. The concept, introduced in Aristotle's *Metaphysics*, was first developed theologically by Thomas Aquinas in his *Summa Theologica*, Cf. Q 3, A, I; Q 9, A, I; Q 25, A, I.

43. This error finds extravagant expression in the romantic Catholic poet Angelicus Silesius. Cf. *CD* 2.1.282.

I know that without me God cannot for a moment be.
He needs perish at once were death to come to me . . .
Naught is but I and Thou, and if we two were not,
Then God is no more God, and heaven itself is naught.

44. Tillich, *Systematic Theology*, vol. 1, 229–30, 251–52.

45. *CD* 2.1.285. Barth can even say that "Man is not a person, but . . . finds what a person is when he finds it in the person of God . . ." Barth ends his discussion of the personal nature of God with the notation that the tendency of Neo-Protestantism both to neutralize the divine being and to project upon it the attributes of human personality is no longer a matter of concern — has become "merely historical" (p. 296). In light of the inclination of both process and some feminist theology to attempt a non-personal conception of God or to impose upon God a "balanced" sexuality, we have to say that, on this issue, Barth's judgment was premature.

46. From an unpublished public lecture at Princeton Theological Seminary in June 1987. Miller's proposal is reminiscent of Von Rad's translation: "I will be there for you" which has a very contemporary ring. Gerhard Von Rad, *Old Testament Theology*, 180.

47. In Althaus this "judgment" is called God's "alien work." Althaus, *Theology of Martin Luther*, 141. See also *Luther's Works*, vol. 2, 134. Elsewhere Luther wrote, "so far as we are concerned, even [God's] works of wrath must be nothing but love." See Seeberg, *History of Doctrines*, bk. 2, 245.

48. *CD* 2.1.280.

49. Sallie McFague, *Metaphorical Theology* (Philadelphia: Fortress Press, 1982), 197.

50. Ibid., 185.

51. Herzog, *Justice Church*, 86.

2. The Structure of Divine Freedom

1. Violence against and among anti-apartheid activists appears to be escalating. Since the release of Nelson Mandella, fighting has broken out between members of Inkatha and the ANC, while white reactionary groups have grown in number and power. As a result, leaders in the struggle against apartheid, both black and white, are increasingly the targets of "hit squads." Frank Chikane, the successor to Byres Naudé as General Secretary of the South African Council of Churches, has recently been the victim of an attempted poisoning, and the home of Ivor Jenkins, National Coordinator for *Koinonia SA*, has been attacked by gunfire.

2. Since the Smith's move into Mamelodi several years ago, there has come into existence an organization called "Koinonia Southern Africa," which has as its primary mission bringing together blacks and whites on a social and theological basis. Koinonia has offices throughout South Africa and representatives in Europe, England, and the United States. See their publication, *Koinonia*, published in Silverton 0127, Pretoria, Republic of South Africa.

3. Immanuel Kant, *Religion Within the Limits of Reason Alone*, trans. T. M. Green and H. H. Hudson (New York: Harper & Row, 1960), 130–31.

4. In this chapter I am interpreting, in some ways *re*interpreting — and on the fourth point, adding to — Barth's discussion of divine freedom and applying it to the question of liberation. Cf. *CD* 2.1.297–350.

5. The description of God's being and action as *a se*, from itself, is found first in Anselm, and is then taken up as the general presupposition of Aquinas's five demonstrations of the existence of God, especially the third which speaks of God as necessary being. See *Summa Theologica*, part 1, quest. 2, art. 3.

6. *CD* 2.1.306.

7. Cf. Reinhold Niebuhr, *The Nature and Destiny of Man*, vol. 1 (New York: Charles Scribner's Sons, 1941), 296ff.; and Paul Tillich, *Love, Power, and Justice* (New York: Oxford University Press, 1960), 1–18.

8. *CD* 2.1.308.

9. Alfred North Whitehead, *Process and Reality* (New York: Macmillan Co., 1929), 523–24.

10. Charles Hartshorne, *The Divine Relativity* (New Haven: Yale University Press, 1948), 138.

11. Gordon D. Kaufman, *Theology for a Nuclear Age* (Philadelphia: Westminster Press, 1985), 42.

12. If the first verse of Genesis is read, "*When* God began to create" [RSV, note a.], the poet's neglect of the *ex nihilo* principle becomes even more apparent, because coincident with God's creation, there is already an "earth . . . without form and void and darkness." The dogmatic implications of the rest of the chapter contradict this reading as well.

13. While the radical monism of Hindu mythology may avoid the problem, a pre-existent reality appears in the Sumerian primordial sea, personified in Tiamat, who in Babylonian mythology becomes the basis of all

108   *The Freedom of God and Human Liberation*

other creation after her defeat by the demiurge Marduk. In Greek mythology, according to Hesiod, Chaos gives rise to a primal earth, which in turn produces all other being, including the gods. In Shintoism there is a primordial sea, which upon being stirred by the gods Izanagi and Izanami, produces an island, "the pillar of the earth," from which all else is created.

14. Plotinus, *The Enneads*, trans. S. MacKenna (London: Faber and Faber, Ltd., 1930), 380.

15. It was a weakness in Calvin's doctrine of providence that his conception of divine freedom moved to a consideration of God's free governance *over* the creation without due regard for his freedom *from* it. As one reads through chaps. 16, 17, and 18 of bk. 1 of the *Institutes*, there is an inescapable impression of being thrust toward a monism in which Calvin's exhaustive description of the dependence of creation upon the creator finally threatens the necessary distinction between them.

16. While this approach is characteristic of all Latin American liberation theology, one thinks especially of Jon Sobrino's *Christology at the Crossroads* (Maryknoll: Orbis Books, 1978). In this connection, it is interesting to note that Barth's 1911 lecture, "Jesus Christ and the Movement for Social Justice," may stand as the earliest example of a revolutionary "Christology from below." It can be found in George Hunsinger's *Karl Barth and Radical Politics* (Philadelphia: Westminster Press, 1976), 19–47.

17. *Institutes* 2. 13, 5.; Cf. also 4. 17. 30.

18. E. R. Hardy and C. C. Richardson, eds., *Christology of the Later Fathers*, The Library of Christian Classics 3 (London: SCM Press, 1954), 218.

19. Peter C. Hodgson, *New Birth of Freedom: A Theology of Bondage and Liberation* (Philadelphia: Fortress Press, 1976), 270, 273.

20. Paul Tillich, *Systematic Theology*, vol. 2 (Chicago: University of Chicago Press, 1957), 60ff.

21. *CD* 2. 1. 314. For the following exposition of this point see 314–15, passim.

22. Again we have reference to the doctrine of the being and work of God *ad extra*. The general irrelevance of the "death of God" movement for the cause of social justice may be traced to its neglect of this concept. The movement's peculiar "kenotic" theology of the emptying (the dying) of God left the reality of God empty of any potentiality or significance for those who suffer oppression.

23. The latter possibility is not without precedent. One thinks of Joachim de Fiore (1132–1202) whose prediction of a liberating "Age of the Spirit" inspired revolutionary activity among the Fratricelli of the fourteenth century.

24. Thomas Merton, *Contemplation in a World of Action* (London: Unwin Paperbacks, 1980), 157ff.

25. Karl Barth, quoted in George Hunsinger, *Karl Barth and Radical Politics* (Philadelphia: Westminster Press, 1975), 84. For more on Barth's socialism see Alexander J. McKelway, "Karl Barth and Politics," in *Perspectives in Religious Studies* 15 (Fall 1988).

26. *CD* 2. 1. 315.

27. *Institutes* 3, 24. 5.

3. Thinking about God

1. Robert P. Scharlemann, "Onto- and Theo-logical Thinking" in *Inscriptions and Reflections* (Charlottesville: University Press of Virginia, 1989), 4.

2. David Hume, *A Treatise on Human Nature*, ed. L. A. Selby-Bigge (Oxford: Clarendon Press, 1888), 196–97.

3. Ludwig Feuerbach, *The Essence of Christianity* (New York: Harper & Row, 1957), 230.

4. Attributed to the sixth-century B.C. philosopher, Xenophanes, who also noted that "Aethiopean gods are black and snub-nosed, Thracian gods have red hair," and, if they could make them, animals "too would have their deities, made like themselves." See Kathleen Freeman, *The Pre-Socratic Philosophers* (Cambridge: Harvard University Press, 1959), 96.

5. Feuerbach, *Essence*, 218.

6. Ibid., 13.

7. John R. Searle, "The World Turned Upside Down," *The New York Review* (Oct. 27, 1983): 74, passim.

8. Colin Campbell, "The Tyranny of the Yale Critics," *The New York Times Magazine* (Feb. 9, 1986): 25.

9. Saussure writes, "In language there are only differences . . . The idea or phonic substance that a sign contains is of less importance than the other signs that surround it." Quoted in Jacques Derrida, *Speech and Phenomena*, trans. David B. Allison (Evanston: Northwestern University Press, 1973), 140.

10. Barbara Johnson agrees that for Derrida, "Language is a system of differences rather than a collection of independently meaningful units . . . language as such is already constituted by the very distance and differences it seeks to overcome." See "Translator's Introduction" in Jacques Derrida, *Dissemination*, trans. Barbara Johnson (Chicago: University of Chicago Press, 1981), ix.

11. Derrida, *Speech* 143.

12. Noted in Searle, "Upside Down," 76. Derrida is speaking of Rousseau's text and states: "*There is nothing outside the text . . .* there has never been anything but writing; there have never been anything but supplements, substitutive significations which could only come forth in a chain of differential references." Jacques Derrida, *On Grammatology*, trans. G. C. Spivak (Baltimore: John's Hopkins University Press, 1974) 158–59.

13. Searle, "Upside Down," 74.

14. Barbara Johnson in Derrida, *Dissemination*, xv.

15. Campbell, "Tyranny," 21.

16. Karl Barth, *The Epistle to the Romans*, trans. Edwyn c. Hoskyns (London: Oxford University Press, 1953), 65, and passim.

17. *CD* 1. 2. 126. Emphasis mine.

18. Karl Barth, *The Word of God and the Word of Man* (Gloucester: Peter Smith, 1978), 45. Emphasis mine.

19. Peter C. Hodgson, review of *Erring* in *Religious Studies Review* 12 (July/October 1986): 256.

20. Mark C. Taylor, *Erring: A Postmodern A/theology*, (Chicago: University of Chicago Press, 1984), 13. "To believe is to have faith in grammar" (p. 80). "God is what word means and word is what God means" (p. 104).

21. Ibid., 168.

22. Hodgson, Review of *Erring*, 257.

23. See note 1.

24. Scharlemann, "Thinking," 4.

25. Scharlemann, "Thinking," 10.

26. The "negative" theology of Cusanus and the Pseudo Dionysius, whereby the formula is reversed and "our not thinking of God" (thinking of God as "not") is proper thinking of God, has been labeled "cataphatic." Barth objects to this tradition on the grounds that it asserts a human capacity for the knowledge of God by way of "revocation and relativization of all the definiteness of the divine nature" (*CD* 2. 1. 193). Of course, his own position bears a certain similarity to the *via negativa* when he claims that ". . . our knowledge of God begins in all seriousness with the knowledge of the hiddenness of God." (p. 183.) The difference lies in the fact that, for Barth, God *"reveals* himself as hidden," for it is nevertheless true that "In his revelation in Jesus Christ, the hidden God has indeed made himself apprehensible." (p. 199).

27. Scharlemann, "Thinking," 10.

28. Jürgen Moltmann, *The Crucified God* (New York: Harper & Row, 1974), 215, as noted in Scharlemann "Thinking," 10. In an earlier essay Scharlemann develops the "not-beingness" of God in terms of trinitarian alterity — God is "another." See Robert Scharlemann, "The Being of God When God Is Not Being God" in *Deconstruction and Theology*, ed. Thomas Altizer et al. (New York: Crossroad, 1982), 90.

29. According to George Hunsinger, Marquardt argued "that Barth was a radical socialist with strong anarchistic tendencies; that his theology not only arose from but aims toward socialist action; that revolution was the basic concept for Barth's understanding of both God and society, [and] that Barth's mature Christology provided the final grounding for leftist convictions arrived at earlier." See George Hunsinger, *Karl Barth and Radical Politics* (Philadelphia: Westminster Press, 1976), 9. Notwithstanding the fact that Marquardt's central thesis is contradicted by both the history and content of Barth's thought, he has rendered considerable service in reminding us of Barth's radical and socialist convictions — which, however, were informed by his theology and not vice versa. For critiques of Marquardt's argument see Eberhard Jüngel, *Karl Barth: A Theological Legacy* (Philadelphia: Westminster Press, 1986) and Alexander J. McKelway, "Karl Barth and Politics," in *Perspectives in Religious Studies* 15 (No. 3, Fall 1988): 269–81.

30. Jüngel, 102.

31. Ibid.

32. Ibid., 95.

33. For an enlightening comparison of the first and second editions of Barth's *Romans*, see Jüngel, 162ff.

34. Barth, *Romans*, 137.

35. Jüngel, *Karl Barth*, 69.

36. Karl Barth, *Anselm: Fides Quaerens Intellectum* (London: SCM Press, 1960), 170.

37. Ibid., 167.

38. Jüngel, *Karl Barth*, 42.

39. *CD* 1. 2. 471.

40. *CD* 2. 1. 156.

41. *CD* 2. 1. 206.

42. *CD* 2. 1. 212.

43. *CD* 2. 1. 188.

44. *CD* 2. 1. 277.

45. *CD* 2. 1. 23.

4. *The Liberating Word*

1. *Institutes* 1. 6. 3.

2. Letty M. Russell, *The Liberating Word: A Guide to Non-Sexist Interpretation of the Bible* (Philadelphia: Westminster Press, 1976), 14, 97.

3. Again, we mean by the last form of God's freedom *not* that God is free from himself or free from his gracious intentions for the creation, but that God is free from any *particular* means by which God accomplishes his purposes — even if such variation of method appears contradictory to us.

4. *Luther's Works*, vol. 35, ed. E. T. Bachmann (Philadelphia: Muhlenberg Press, 1960), 236.

5. Calvin often employed the optical metaphors of focus and reflection. Scriptures are "spectacles" by which "otherwise confused knowledge of God" is brought into focus. Cf. *Institutes* 1. 6. 1. He can also speak of the Old Testament — specifically Deuteronomy 32 — as "a bright mirror in which God is manifest" (1. 8. 7.) and, generally, "the Word itself, however it be imparted to us, is like a mirror in which faith may contemplate God" (3. 2. 6.). The same must hold true for the Word made flesh. "Christ, then, is the mirror wherein we must, and without self-deception may, contemplate our own election" (3. 24. 5.). In a beautiful if also unusual passage, Calvin, commenting upon Ps. 8:2, asserts that not only is scripture a "clear mirror of God's works . . . in human kind, but that infants, while they nurse at their mother's breasts, have tongues so eloquent to preach [God's] glory that there is no need at all for other orators" (1. 5. 3.). It is, for Calvin, the finite *humanity* of the Bible that makes it an instrument fit for revelation.

6. John Calvin, *Treatises Against the Anabaptists and Against the Libertines*, trans. and ed. Benjamin Wirt Farley, (Grand Rapids: Baker Book House, 1982), 214–15. "For who even of slight intelligence does not understand that, as nurses commonly do with infants, God is wont in a measure to 'lisp' in speaking to us?" (*Institutes* 1. 13. 1).

7. *CD* 1. 2. 499. The reference is to Calvin's *Institutes* 3. 11. 9.

8. *CD* 1. 2. 500.

9. *CD* 1. 2. 32.

10. Ernst Käsemann, *Jesus Means Freedom* (London: SCM Press, 1969), 9.

11. Rosemary Radford Ruether, *Sexism and God Talk: Toward a Feminist Theology* (Boston: Beacon Press, 1983), 23.

12. *Institutes* 1. 7. 5. Calvin goes on at the same place as if to respond to his more modern critics: We hold this view of scripture, "not as persons accustomed to seize upon some unknown thing . . . fully conscious that we hold the unassailable truth! Nor do we do this as those miserable men who habitually bind over their minds to the thralldom of superstition; but we feel that the undoubted power of his divine majesty lives and breathes there."

13. Cf. *The Westminster Confession*, chap. 1, par. 9, and *The Second Helvetic Confession*, chap. 2, par. 1, in *Creeds of the Churches*, ed. John H. Leith (Richmond: John Knox Press, 1973), 196, 135.

14. *CD* 1. 1. 26.

15. Geoffrey Galt Harpham, *The Ascetic Imperative in Culture and Criticism* (Chicago: University of Chicago Press, 1987), 137.

16. Paul Tillich, *Systematic Theology*, vol. 1 (Chicago: University of Chicago Press, 1951), 227.

17. Ibid., 133.

18. Cf. Jon Sobrino, *Christology at the Crossroads* (Maryknoll: Orbis Books, 1984), 50, 60, 292.

19. Cf. Gustavo Gutiérrez, *A Theology of Liberation* (Maryknoll: Orbis Books, 1973), 13.

20. Gustavo Gutiérrez, *The Power of the Poor in History* (Maryknoll: Orbis Books, 1983), 69.

21. Archibald A. Hodge and Benjamin B. Warfield, "Inspiration," *Presbyterian Review* (April 1881), cited in *American Christianity*, ed. H. Shelton Smith, Robert T. Handy and Lefferts A. Loetscher (New York: Charles Scribner's Sons, 1963), 332.

22. Hodge and Warfield "Inspiration," in *American Christianity* pp. 326–27. Emphasis mine.

23. Hodge and Warfield "Inspiration," in *American Christianity*, p. 328.

24. For a useful summary of "Scottish Realism" see Sydney E. Ahlstrom, "Scottish Philosophy and American Theology," *Church History* 24 (No. 3, Sept. 1955): 257–72. Emerging from the "moderate" wing of Scottish Presbyterianism in the eighteenth century, this school (sometimes referred to as "Common Sense Philosophy") sought to counter the religious skepticism of Hume's empiricism by asserting the following: (1) philosophy begins with "scientific observation of self-consciousness" which, as such, is not subject to Newtonian laws; (2) by such inner "observation" certain principles of knowledge can be established (e.g., cause and effect constitutes a "necessary" principle, while " the existence of a thing perceived" constitutes a "contingent" principle); (3) only an intelligent being can be an efficient cause (thus denying materialism); (4) the first principles of morals are self-evident intuitions (p. 261). While this philosophy had an impact upon early nineteenth century liberalism in America (e.g., William Channing, Nathaniel Taylor), its influence can also be seen in American fundamentalism — as in the "Princeton Theology" developed through the line of John Witherspoon, Archibald Alexander, and Charles Hodge. Hodge's *Systematic Theology* betrayed the anthropocentrism of Scottish

Realism (even, according to one Dutch critic, "the stain of humanism") by appealing to that school's principle of reason to reconcile the problem of human freedom and divine sovereignty. In respect to biblical authority, a theory of infallibility was constructed by the younger A. A. Hodge on the basis of the principle of cause and effect, which operated independently of sense experience and could become the basis of assumptions concerning "original autographs." Finally, for the Princeton theologians, faith itself was tested by inner disposition more than by biblical or confessional agreement. "Self-consciousness became the oracle of religious truth" (p. 269). Thus was completed the circle binding together rationalism, liberalism, fundamentalism, and modern evangelicalism.

25. Elizabeth Schüssler Fiorenza, *In Memory of Her: A Feminist Theological Reconstruction of Christian Origins* (New York: Crossroad, 1983), 30.

26. Elizabeth Schüssler Fiorenza, *Bread Not Stone: The Challenge of Feminist Biblical Interpretation* (Boston: Beacon Press, 1984), 20ff.

27. Elizabeth Schüssler Fiorenza, "Interpreting Patriarchal Traditions," in Russell, *Liberating Word*, 61.

28. *An Inclusive Language Lectionary*, ed. the Inclusive Language Lectionary Committee of the Division of Education and Ministry, the National Council of the Churches of Christ in the U.S.A. (Philadelphia: Westminster Press, 1983).

29. Paul L. Lehmann, *The Decalogue*, (manuscript), chap. 4, p. 155.

30. Roland Frye decries both literalists and those who find the Bible in need of correction. "Both represent an anachronistic extension of the narrowest vision of an earlier age, and of its down-playing of the metaphor . . . — which leads the one group in effect to accept everything in the Bible as literally univocal with reality, and the other to reject anything in the Bible which does not appear to them to be so." See Roland M. Frye, "Metaphors, Equations, and the Faith," *Theology Today* 37 (April 1980): 64.

31. *Lectionary*, "Appendix," 3; "Introduction," 4.

32. *Lectionary*, "Introduction," 2; "Appendix," 6, 8.

33. *Lectionary*, Pentecost 16 and Christmas Day, Second Proper.

34. Noted in Roland M. Frye, *Language of God and Feminist Lanuage: Problems and Principles* in *The Scottish Journal of Theology* vol. 41, no. 4, 1988, 441–469. Professor Frye's essay offers perhaps the most comprehensive literary critique of feminist "God language" available.

35. Notwithstanding the common definition of "lectionary" as "a list of lessons from scripture," the Inclusive Language Lectionary Committee openly distinguishes its text from the Bible. "It does not supplant the Bible. The Bible is the church's book . . . A lectionary is also the church's book" (*Lectionary*, "Introduction," 1). If, as is here admitted, this collection of readings is something other than a re-presentation of the biblical text, and if, as is intended, these readings are to be used in place of the Revised Standard Version in the worship of the church, then it is difficult to see how the Bible is not there and then "supplanted."

36. While the issue cannot be pursued here, it ought to be noted that the Bible may be subjected to a different sort of literalism, namely, from historical, textual, and other forms of criticism when those investigations seeks to

marginalize certain biblical texts in favor of others thought to be more authentic. A case in point might be Peter C. Hodgson's objection in his *New Birth of Freedom* . . . to James Cone's assertion in *A Black Theology of Liberation* that "Jesus himself defines the nature of his ministry" in the words of Luke. 4:18–19: "He has sent me to proclaim release to the captives." Hodgson complains that "it is clear to critical scholarship that those words are the construction of the Evangelist . . . liberation theology simply must work more critically with biblical texts" (p. 209). By this method, Hodgson believes, liberation theologians will have at their disposal "more authentic sayings or actions of Jesus" (p. 210). One would have thought that after Barth and Ricoeur we would be long past that kind of critical literalism — as if historical and textual criticism could reproduce Jesus' "authentic" speech and action — as if we were not invited and required to enter the thought-world of the text — as if we had at our disposal a different or better word than that offered by the text itself. Professor Cone knows that the liberating word of God is found in the church's canon, and not in the latest findings of "critical scholarship."

37. Whether this is an apt description of the religious disposition and political role of Mikhail S. Gorbachev is matter of considerable debate.

38. "The infallible rule of interpretation of scripture, is the scripture itself; and therefore, when there is a question about the true and full sense of any scripture (which is not manifold, but one), it may be searched and known by other places that speak more clearly." (*Westminster Confession of Faith*), chap. 1, par. 9.

39. John R. Searle, "The World Turned Upside Down," *The New York Review* (October 27, 1983): 74.

40. Lehmann, *Decalogue*, ms. 128.

41. Cf. Num. 23:19, I Sam. 15:29, and conversely, Ezek. 28:2, 9.

42. Mary Daly, "The Qualitative Leap Beyond Patriarchal Religion," *Quest* 1 (Women and Spirituality, 1974): 21.

43. Frye, *Language of God*, 15, 20.

44. Ibid., 19.

45. Ibid., 19–20.

46. Paul D. Hanson, "Translating, Preaching, and Our Words for God" in *The Hermeneutical Quest*, ed. Donald G. Miller (Allison Park: Pickwick Publications, 1986), 168.

47. *CD* 2. 1. 129–30.

48. Schüssler Fiorenza, *In Memory of Her*, 151.

49. Lehmann, *Decalogue*, ms. 151.

5. Liberating Theology

1. Gustavo Gutiérrez, *A Theology of Liberation* (Maryknoll: Orbis Books, 1973), 15.

2. Leonardo and Clodovis Boff, *Introducing Liberation Theology* (Maryknoll: Orbis Books, 1988), 12. Here the demand, so often found in liberation

theology, that praxis precede reflection, seems to be reversed or at least gives way to correlation.

3. Cf. Allan Boesak, *Farewell to Innocence* (Maryknoll: Orbis Books, 1984), 90–91; and Charles Villa-Vicencio, *Between Christ and Caesar* (Grand Rapids: Wm. B. Eerdmans, 1986), xiii, xxi. Professor Villa-Vicencio's Institute for Contextual Theology in Cape Town, SA, owes much to the "contextual ethics" developed by Paul Lehmann. Of Lehmann's "theological imperative [toward] a political option transcending both tyranny and anarchy," Villa-Vicencio writes: "In celebrating this imperative Professor Lehmann's writings have for many years inspired, disturbed, and shaped my theological pilgrimage" (xiii).

4. *Institutes* 4. 1. 2.

5. Quoted in *Reformed Theology in America*, ed. David F. Wells (Grand Rapids: Wm. B. Eerdmans, 1985), 68.

6. Ibid.

7. *The Book of Confessions* (New York: Office of the General Assembly of the Presbyterian Church USA, 1983), 8. 12.

8. See Susan Schnur's review of Rosemary Radford Ruether's *Women-Church* in *New York Times Book Review* (December 21, 1986): 23.

9. See chap. 1, n. 31.

10. Dorothee Soelle, *Political Theology*, trans. John Shelley (Philadelphia: Fortress Press, 1974), 59.

11. Ibid., 76.

12. Quoted in Klaus Scholder, *The Churches and the Third Reich*, vol. 1, trans. John Bowden (Philadelphia: Fortress Press, 1988), 104.

13. Eberhard Jüngel, *Karl Barth: A Theological Legacy* (Philadelphia: Westminster Press, 1986), 104.

14. Ibid., 102, 103.

15. Boesak, *Farewell to Innocence*, 102.

16. Dorothy Nelkin, *The Creation Controversy* (New York: W. W. Norton & Co., 1982), 76.

17. Ibid., 75.

18. John de Gruchy, *The Church Struggle in South Africa* (Grand Rapids: Wm. B. Eerdmans, 1979), 6.

19. See, for instance, Calvin's praise of pagan astronomers in his *Commentaries*, The Library of Christian Classics 23. (Philadelphia: Westminster Press, 1957), 356, and his commendation of pre-Christian jurists, philosophers, and physicians in *Institutes* 2. 2. 15.

20. Abraham Kuyper, *Calvinism* (Grand Rapids: Wm. B. Eerdmans, 1943), 123.

21. Ibid., 84.

22. de Gruchy, *Church Struggle*, 30.

23. Ibid., 32.

24. Claude Welch, *Protestant Thought in the Nineteenth Century*, vol. 1, (New Haven: Yale University Press, 1972), 59. Welch goes on to describe the turn toward the self by which Schleiermacher and others sought to provide theology with a subject matter more in keeping with the requirements of nineteenth-century intellectual life.

25. *CD* 1. 1. 10.

26. *Annual Meeting Program*, American Academy of Religion, Chicago, November 19–22, 1988.

27. Robert H. Schuller, a minister of the Reformed Church in America, built a large glass-walled church in Garden Grove, a suburb of Los Angeles, California, known as the Crystal Cathedral. Dr. Schuller is famous for his "Hour of Power" television program and for his "positive" interpretation of Christian faith — which closely resembles that of Norman Vincent Peale. Cf. Dennis Voskuil, *Mountains Into Goldmines: Robert Schuller and the Gospel of Success* (Grand Rapids: Wm. B. Eerdmans, 1983), 13ff.

28. David Tracy, "Tillich and Contemporary Theology," in *The Thought of Paul Tillich* ed. J. L. Adams, W. Pauck, and R. L. Shinn (San Francisco: Harper & Row, 1985), 260–75.

29. Francis Fukuyama, "The End of History?," in *The National Interest*, Summer 1989, 3–18. On Fukuyama's account we need not expect further significant development. Cf. Richard Bernstein, "Judging 'Post-History,' The Theory to End All Theories," *The New York Times*, (August 27, 1989).

30. Thomas J. J. Altizer, Joseph Prabhu, et al., "On Deconstructing Theology: A Symposium on *Erring: A Postmodern A/theology*," in the *Journal of the American Academy of Religion* 54 (Fall 1986): 525.

31. Ibid., 537, 543.

32. Letter from John Odom to W. Trent Foley. Used by permission.

33. Wells, *Reformed Theology*, 17.

34. Martin Luther, "The Freedom of the Christian," in *Martin Luther: Selections from His Writings*, ed. John Dillenberger (Garden City: Doubleday, 1961), esp. 69ff. Luther here demonstrates his dependence upon Augustine's dialectic of obedience and freedom and his concept of a "determined freedom."

35. Cf. *CD* 2. 2. x., passim.

36. *The Christian Century* (April 27, 1988): 424–25.

37. *The Christian Century* (Nov. 18, 1987): 1020–21. In June 1989 the board was censured by the American Association of University Professors.

38. Patrick D. Miller, "Forward," in Nancy A. Hardesty, *Inclusive Language in the Church* (Philadelphia: Westminster Press, 1986), 2.

39. Rosemary Radford Ruether, *Women-Church: Theology and Practice of Feminist Liturgical Communities* (San Francisco: Harper & Row, 1985), 6.

40. Ibid., 188ff.

41. Ibid. As it stands, one would have to say that there is as little reason for *liturgical* recognition of a girl's first menstruation as for a boy's first wet dream.

42. Daniel Migliore, "Reappraising Barth's Theology," *Theology Today* vol. XLIII, no. 3 (October 1986): 313.

43. *Institutes* 1. 14. 1. The same story is told by Augustine in his *Confessions*, bk. 11, chap. 12, trans. Rex Warner (New York: New American Library, 1963), 266.

44. *Institutes* 1. 3/4. 7. There is as well a certain *reductio ad absurdum* hilarity in Calvin's use of invective against his theological antagonists who are alternately "beasts," "brutes," "mad-dogs," "asses," "swine," "pests," "vermin," "monsters," etc., etc. Cf. Calvin's *Treatises*, passim.

45. Eberhard Busch, *Karl Barth: His Life from Letters and Autobiographical Texts* (Philadelphia: Fortress Press, 1975), 470.

46. Ibid., 449. It remained for Barth to send word to the dying Brunner: "And tell him *yes*, that the time when I thought I had to say no to him is now long past, since we all live only by virtue of the fact that a great and merciful God says his gracious yes to all of us." (Ibid., 476–77).

47. Migliore, "Reappraising," 313.

48. Ruether, *Women-Church*, 153. The inevitable effect of such sentiments on either sex is disturbingly indicated by the fact that, in my college library's copy of Ruether's book, the aforementioned page was torn down the middle.

49. Cf. Alexander J. McKelway, "Old Myths and a New Reality," *Atlanta Constitution* (January 13, 1989).

50. Elinor Brecher and Robert Garret, "Marilyn's Thieme," *The New Republic* (November 14, 1988): 23. This and other weirdness of the "second family's" religious views gives further cause for the churches to pray for the health and safety of the president.

51. Jüngel, *Karl Barth*, 38.

52. Karl Barth, *Evangelical Theology: An Introduction* (New York: Holt, Reinhart and Winston, 1963), 165.

53. John Hick, ed., *The Myth of God Incarnate* (Philadelphia: Westminster Press, 1977), 167ff. These views caused resistance to Professor Hick's application for membership in the Presbytery of San Gabriel, California. Hick's application was at first accepted by the Presbytery, but upon appeal to the Presbyterian General Assembly, it was rescinded. The case was returned to the San Gabriel Presbytery, and the ensuing trial and debate resulted in Hick's withdrawing his application.

54. E. David Willis, "The Incarnate Word and the Confessing Church Today: Memorandum for San Gabriel Presbytery," Minutes of San Gabriel Presbytery (January 13, 1987): 7.

55. Reinhold Niebuhr, *The Nature and Destiny of Man*, vol. 1 (New York: Charles Scribner's Sons, 1941), 208.

56. Martin Luther, "Two Kinds of Righteousness," in Dillenberger, *Martin Luther*, 86ff.

57. *CD* 2. 1. 387.

58. "The Kairos Document," in *The Kairos Covenant*, ed. Willis H. Logan (New York: Friendship Press, 1988), 16ff. The document rightly rejects calls for reconciliation that do not demand justice, that want peace at any price (p. 18). But a faith built upon the paradox of sin and grace (*simul justus et peccator*) must surely accept the possibility that one can violently resist oppression and at the same time (*simul*) seek reconciliation with the oppressor.

59. *CD* 2. 1. 387.

5. Revolutionary Freedom

1. Cf. Reinhold Niebuhr, *The Children of Light and the Children of Darkness* (New York: Charles Scribner's Sons, 1944), 59f.; *Faith and History* (New York: Charles Scribner's Sons, 1949), 209ff.; *The Nature and Destiny of Man*, vol. 1

118   *The Freedom of God and Human Liberation*

(New York: Charles Scribner's Sons, 1941), 51. Also Karl Barth, *The Epistle to the Romans*, trans. Edwyn C. Hoskyns (London: Oxford University Press, 1933), 481ff.; Paul Tillich, *Systematic Theology*, vols. 1 & 2 (Chicago: University of Chicago Press, 1951, 1957), 1.87, 2.65–66; Paul Lehmann, *The Transfiguration of Politics* (New York: Harper & Row, 1975), chap. 5, esp. 68ff.

2. Niebuhr, *Faith and History*, 209–10.

3. Elena Bonner, *Alone Together* (New York: Alfred Knopf, 1986), cited in John Updike's review in *The New Yorker* (Jan. 19, 1987): 90.

4. Ibid.

5. Eberhard Jüngel, *Karl Barth: A Theological Legacy* (Philadelphia: Westminster Press, 1986), 102.

6. Barth, *Romans*, 481–82.

7. Jüngel, *Karl Barth*, 102.

8. Paul Lehmann, "Karl Barth, Theologian of Permanent Revolution," *Union Seminary Quarterly Review* 28. (Fall 1972); 80.

9. Jürgen Moltmann, *Religion, Revolution, and the Future*, trans. M. D. Meeks (New York: Charles Scribner's Sons, 1969), 131. Cited in Lehmann, "Karl Barth," 80.

10. Fyodor Dostoevsky, *Notes From Underground and The Grand Inquisitor*, trans. R. E. Matlaw (New York: E. P. Dutton, 1960), 123ff.

11. Ibid., 135.

12. Ibid., 139.

13. See K. C. Cole, "A Theory of Everything," *New York Times Magazine* (Oct. 18, 1987): 20–26.

14. "That freedom must be delivered and that this deliverance is deliverance from self-enslavement cannot be said directly; yet it is the central theme of 'salvation,'" Paul Ricoeur, *The Symbolism of Evil*, trans. Emerson Buchanan (Boston: Beacon Press, 1969), 152.

15. Dostoevsky, *Notes*, 130.

16. *CD* 1. 2. 688.

17. Eberhard Busch, "Memories of Karl Barth," in *How Barth Changed My Mind*, ed. Donald K. McKim (Grand Rapids: Wm. B. Eerdmans, 1986), 13.

18. *CD* 4. 1. 101.

19. Barth, *Romans*, 482.

20. R.Pascal in *The Social Basis of the Reformation* (London: Watts and Co., 1933), maintained that Luther was "body and soul" a "petty bourgeois" (p. 194), which is probably taking the point too far.

21. Karl Barth, *The German Church Conflict* (Richmond: John Knox Press, 1965), 30ff.

22. Lehmann, *Transfiguration*, 271. Peter Hodgson objects to what he calls the "apocalyptic" and "suprahistorical" elements in Lehmann's view of the divine revolution, for they provide "too narrow and undialectical a model for understanding the process by which liberation occurs in history." Hodgson calls for a "philosophical basis for understanding the 'new birth' of freedom as a supremely historical event." See Peter C. Hodgson, *New Birth of Freedom: A Theology of Bondage and Liberation* (Philadelphia: Fortress Press, 1976), 283. From our perspective, Hodgson's project, based as it is upon Hegel's philosophy of history, forfeits the redemptively "new thing" that "trans-

figuration" implies. The freedom of God is not trapped in a Hegelian dialectical process which, in its Marxist form, has not, in fact, produced real freedom.

23. Karl Barth, *The Humanity of God* (Richmond: John Knox Press, 1960), 75. Barth said the same thing forty years earlier. "Not by virtue of our own freedom are we what we are; but rather we are what we are not — by the freedom of God" (Barth, *Romans*, 237).

24. Jüngel, *Karl Barth*, 99.

25. Dietrich Bonhoeffer, *Ethics*, ed. Eberhard Bethge (New York: Macmillan Publishing Co., 1965), 29.

26. Letty M.Russell, *Human Liberation in a Feminist Perspective* (Philadelphia: Westminster Press, 1974), 30.

27. While he might object to this unusual employment of "heteronomy," Peter Hodgson appears to be in basic agreement with the general point. For him, freedom creates a "subjectivity" which "is above all *non-autonomous*, because it is based on the 'free life' brought into the world and made a presently efficacious reality by the One who *is* the resurrection and the life" (Hodgson, *New Birth*, 344). Such freedom is "other" oriented; it is "non-separated" and "non-alienated" (399ff.).

28. Barth, *Humanity of God*, 78–79.

INDEX

a se, 107 n 5
Abraham, 58, 63, 65, 67
Absence, 41, 43–44, 81
Actual entities, 20
ad extra, 24, 108 n 13
Africa, 27
Afrikaner, 76, 86, 88, 94
Ahlstrom, Sydney E., 112 n 24
Alexander, Archibald, 112 n 24
Althaus, Paul, 74, 105 n 28, 106 n 47
Altizer, Thomas, 78, 116 n 30
America, 4, 70, 73, 78, 82–83, 90, 97,
    112 n 24, 116 n 27; civil religion, 4;
    foreign policy, 10; form of govern-
    ment, 27; civil war, 72; Academy of
    Religion, 77, 116 n 26; Association of
    University Professors, 116 n 37
analogia, entis, 50, 106 n 39; *attribu-
    tionis*, 51; *gracie*, 51
Analogy, 50–52; of faith (*analogia fidei*),
    39, 47, 49, 51
Anderson, Bernard W., 106 n 41
Androcentrism, 62
Androgyny, 65
Anselm, 49–50, 107 n 5, 111 n 37
Anthropocentrism, 112 n 24
Anthropomorphism, 8, 18
Anti-Semitism, 2, 85
Apartheid, 75–76, 86, 107 n 1
Apocrypha, 62
Apophatic, 43
Apostles, 55
Apollinarius, 22
Aquinas, Thomas, 6, 106 n 42, 107 n 5
Aristotle, 34, 50, 106 n 42
Arius, 30
Arminius, Jacob, 15
Aryan nation, 73
Aseity, 3, 19–20, 50, 89, 96
Atheist, 49
Atonement, 39
Augustine, 81, 116 nn 34 and 43
Authority, 9, 39, 57, 61, 63, 73–74, 85,
    87–88, 92, 95, 99–101, 113 n 24;

Autonomy, 89–91, 93–102

Bainton, 105 nn 25 and 29
Balaam, 64, 66
Baptist, John 57
Barmen, 59, 71, 73
Barth, Karl, 1, 3–5, 7, 11–13, 19, 28, 30,
    33, 39, 42, 47–51, 55, 57, 67, 70, 71,
    74, 76, 78, 81, 83, 86, 89, 90–91, 95,
    98–99, 104 n 2, 105 nn 16 and 23,
    106 nn 40 and 45, 107 n 4, 108 nn 16
    and 25, 109 nn 16 and 18, 110 nn 26,
    29, 34, 111 nn 35–36 and 38, 114 n 36,
    115 n 13, 116 n 42, 117 nn 45–46 and
    51–52, 118 nn 16, 18, 19 and 21,
    119 nn 23 and 28
Basel, 70
Beauty, 33–35, 41, 45
Being, 12, 43, 46, 49–51; of God, 8, 13,
    39, 45, 51–52, 106 n 39
Bergson, 23
Berkeley, George, 35
Bernstein, Richard, 116 n 29
Bible, 1, 13, 20, 36–37, 42–43, 51, 53–54,
    56–67, 72, 75, 88–89, 111 n 5, 113 nn
    30 and 36
Biko, Steven, 87
Bill of Rights, 90
Black, 107 n 1, 109 n 4; Americans, 97;
    blacks, 4, 7, 59, 72, 90, 107 n 2
Body, 118 n 20
Boesak, Allan, 10, 71, 74, 86, 105 n 34,
    115 nn 3 and 15
Boff, Leonardo and Clodovis, 71, 114 n
    2
Bondage, 1, 22, 30, 38, 99–102
Bonhoeffer, Dietrich, 87, 100–101,
    119 n 25
Bonner, Elena, 90, 118 n 3
Bourgeoisie, 15, 96, 118 n 20
Botha, 107 n 1
Brahms, Johannes, 42
Brecher, Elinor, 117 n 50
Broyler, Gil, 104 n 8

Brunner, Emil, 13, 81, 117 n 46
Buddhism, 78
Bultman, Rudolf, 81
burakumin, 104 n 10
Busch, Eberhard, 11, 95–96, 106 nn
  37–38, 117 n 45, 118 n 17
Bush, George, 82

Capitalism, 29, 59, 74, 82
Calvin, John, 5, 8, 15, 24, 31, 55, 71, 75,
  78–79, 81, 104 n 5, 105 n 36, 108 n 15,
  111 nn 5–7, 112 n 12, 115 n 19, 116 n
  44
Cambodia, 90
Campbell, Colin, 109 nn 15, 18
Canon, 65, 114 n 36
Cataphatic, 110 n 26
Catechesis/catechumens, 70
Categories, 8, 35–36, 82, 95
Causation, 19, 35, 42
Central America, 17
Channing, William, 112 n 24
Chauvinism, 65, 73
Chikane, Frank, 107 n 1
Child, 63, 91, abuse, 26
China, 76, 98
Christ, Carol, 4, 104 n 9
Christian community, 1, 5
Christmas, 62
Christocentricity, 3
Christology, 3–4, 21, 77, 104 n 7, 110 n
  29; from below, 23, 108 n 16
Church, 1–2, 8, 10, 26, 33, 61–63, 65, 67,
  71–73, 75, 77, 79–80, 84–86, 89, 92,
  96–97, 101, 114 n 36, 116 n 27;
  Presbyterian, 72; Dutch Reformed,
  75; medieval, 8, 78; German, 74;
  Reformed in America, 116 n 27
Civil rights, 91, 104 n 10
Classical realism, 34, 36, 82
Cold War, 83, 97
Cole, K. C., 118 n 13
Commandments, 65
Common Sense Philosophy, 112 n 24
Communism, 22, 27, 59, 74, 78, 82, 83,
  93
Community, 9, 15, 26, 27, 63, 74, 82
Cone, James, 4, 79, 114 n 36
Conscience, 85
Consumerism, 77–78, 82
Contextual ethics, 115 n 3
Conversion, 37
Courage, 83–84, 86–87, 93

Creation, 13, 18–19, 21–24, 26–28, 30–
  31, 81, 102, 107 n 12, 108 n 15, 111
  n 3; out of nothing (*creatio ex nihilo*),
  20–21; myths, 21
Creationists, 75
Creator, 12, 28, 99, 108 n 13
Cross, 8–9, 24
Crowley, Robert, 79
Crucifixion, 57
Culler, Robert, 41
Cult, 64–65
Culture, 4, 9–10, 15, 26, 29, 43, 63, 74,
  91
Curran, Charles, 79
Cusanus, Nicholas, 110 n 16
Crusades, 62
Crystal Cathedral, 116 n 27

Daly, Mary, 65, 114 n 42
Daughter/daughters, 54, 74, 82, 106 n
  36
de Fiore, Joachim, 108 n 23
de Grunchy, John, 115 nn 18 and 22
de Klerk, 107 n 1
de Saussure, Ferdinand, 41
Death, 9, 23, 31, 38–39, 47, 84, 87, 101,
  106 n 43
Deconstruction, 38, 40–45, 65, 78
Democracy, 2, 5, 17, 69, 83, 92, 98;
  socialist, 27
Derrida, Jacques, 40–42, 63, 65, 109 nn
  9–12 and 14
Destiny, 13, 75, 98; manifest, 75
Determinisim, 93, 95
Devil, 48, 70
Dialectic/dialectical, 8, 26–29, 50, 116 n
  34
Dialectical process, 119 n 22
Differance, 41
Difference, 37, 41–43, 48
Ding an sich, 35
Discipleship, 23, 102
Divine, selfhood, 19; immanence, 23;
  milieu, 44, sovereignty, 9, 113 n 24
Docetic, 56
Dogmatics, 70–71
Dostoevsky, 91–95, 99, 118 nn 10 and
  15
Dukakis, Michael, 83

Eastern Europe, 2, 17, 22, 29, 69, 82, 92
Ecclesiology, 80
Ecology, 73

Economy, 40, 93; free market, 98
Either/or, 100
Election, 24, 78
Empiricism, 75, 112 n 24
England, 107 n 2
Enlightenment, 76
Epistemology, 48
eta, 104 n 10
Eternity, 11
Ethics, 56, 100; prudential, 100
Europe, 71, 76, 107 n 2
Evangelism, 4, 113 n 24
Evangelist, 114 n 36
Evil, 92–93
ex nihilo, 107 n 12
Existence, 11, 20, 25, 27, 35, 39, 48–49,
    5, 94, 100, 112 n 24; human exist-
    ence, 6, 20, 31, 55; of God, 7, 12, 43,
    48, 49, 50, 107 n 5; creaturely, 28, 42
Extra Calvinisticum, 24

Faith, 1–2, 12, 22, 29, 31, 36–37, 46–49,
    51, 53, 57–58, 63–64, 71, 74, 77, 80,
    83, 85–87, 100–101, 110 n 20, 111 n 5,
    113 n 24, 117 n 58; Christian 2, 96,
    116 n 27; reformed, 78
Fall, 25
Family, 26, 75; nuclear, 27
Father, 11, 15, 66–67, 70, 84, 94, 102,
    105–106 n 36; heavenly, 67
Female, 11, 63, 65, 67; imagery, 66
Feminism, 69, 104 n 10; feminist inter-
    pretation, 66
Feuerbach, L., 6, 38–40, 43–44, 104 n
    16, 109 nn 3 and 5
finitum non capax infinitum, 21
Fiction, 105 n 31
Fiorenza, Elizabeth Schüssler, 62, 67,
    113 nn 25–27, 114 n 48
Flesh, 1, 23, 30, 51, 54–55, 57, 111 n 5
Foley, W. Trent, 116 n 32
Forgiveness, 84–85; of sins, 9, 47, 86
Fratricelli, 108 n 23
Freedom of God, in himself, 3, 9–10,
    20, 22, 23, 29, 50, 52, 54, 56, 60, 88;
    from other being, 18, 20, 22–23, 29–
    30, 60, 88; for us (*pro nobis*), 3, 8, 14,
    18, 22, 23, 27, 29–30, 50, 54–55, 63,
    88; from his freedom for, 18, 27,
    29–30, 60, 88
Freeman, Kathleen, 109 n 4
Frye, Roland, 66, 113 nn 30, 34, 114 n
    43

Fukuyama, Francis, 78, 116 n 29
Fundamentalism, 60–62, 75, 79, 112 n
    24, 113 n 24

Gadamer, 63
Garret, Robert, 117 n 50
Gender, 65
General Assembly, 105 n 33
Genius, 43
German Christian, 4; Reformation, 96
Germany, 17
glasnost, 83
God, image of, 4, 33, 65, 67; as pure
    being, 5; as being itself, 5, 12, 45; as
    the ground or power of being, 5, 45;
    as action, 5; as love, 5, 14; as he is in
    himself, 5, 14, 44; God above God, 6;
    as truth itself, 6; as beauty itself, 6; as
    justice itself, 6; as prime mover, 6; as
    first cause, 6; as necessary being, 6;
    as the maximum being, 6; as univer-
    sal designer, 6; as finite, 6; as immut-
    able, 6; as invisible, 6; humanity of,
    8, 18; as friend 8, 15; as companion,
    8; as partner, 8; as Father, 11, 46, 62,
    66; as God, 11, 14, 16, 18, 52, 77, 84;
    as one who acts, 12; as one who acts
    in love, 12; God is God, 12–13, 14, 96;
    as *actus purus* (pure act), 13; as living,
    13; as personal, 13; as person, 13; as
    one who loves, 14; as maximal being,
    20; death of, 24, 43, 71, 77–78, 108
    n 22; God incarnate, 25; as writing,
    43; as king, 46; as son of Mary, 46; as
    the crucified, 46; as Creator, 53; as
    Liberator, 53; as Advocate, 53; as a
    woman in travail, 66; man of war, 66;
    as mother eagle, 66
gods, 38–39, 108 n 13, 109 n 4
Goddess, 78
Goodness, 35, 41, 82, 102
Gospel, 23, 38, 46, 53, 59, 64, 69, 72, 74,
    97, 99–100
Gorbachev, Michail, 114 n 37
Government, 5, 40, 90
Grace, 5, 11, 23, 26–27, 31, 51, 54,
    63–64, 67, 79, 81–82, 85–86, 98–101,
    106 n 36, 117 n 58; common, 75
Grand Inquisitor, 91–92, 94–95, 99
Gregory of Nazianzus, 25
Guilt, 31, 39, 87, 101; consciousness,
    85
Grünwald, 57

Gutiérrez, Gustavo, 4, 59, 69, 79, 112 nn 19–20, 114 n 1

Hagar, 65, 67
Hanson, Paul, 66, 114 n 46
Hardesty, Nancy, 79, 116 n 38
Harpham, Geoffrey, 57, 112 n 15
Hartshorne, Charles, 20, 23, 107 n 110
Hegel, G. W. F., 7, 23, 25, 78, 88, 105 n 22
Hell, 81
Hermeneutic, 59–60, 62; of suspicion, 59; of revolutionary praxis, 59; political, 59; feminist, 64
Herzog, Frederick, 15, 105 n 32, 107 n 51
Hesiod, 108 n 13
Heteronomy, 101, 119 n 27; heteronomous freedom, 102
Heterosexuals, 4
Hick, John, 84, 117 n 53
Hindu mythology, 107 n 13
Hirsch, Immanuel, 97
Historical, process, 9; critical school, 70; criticism, 71, 114 n 36
History, 23, 25–26, 29, 33, 42, 60, 62–64, 69, 72, 88, 90–91, 96–97, 102, 110 n 29, 118 n 22; of religions, 76; of Christian thought, 82; historiography, 76
Hodge, A. A. 60–62, 112 nn 21–23, 113 n 24
Hodge, Charles, 78, 112 n 24
Hodgson, Peter, 26, 43–44, 108 n 19, 110 nn 19 and 22, 114 n 36, 118 n 22, 119 n 27
homoousia, 8
Homosexuals, 4, 79
Human, community, 4; being, 6, 8–9, 19, 21, 24, 26, 40, 43, 48–49, 92, 106 n 39; nature, 6–7, 39, 43, 82; responsibility, 21; rights, 90
Humanism, 113 n 24; Christian, 93
Hume, David, 34–35, 109 n 2
Humor, 70, 80–81
Hunsinger, George, 108 nn 16 and 25, 110 n 29

I/Thou, 13
Ideology/ideological, 10–11, 73–76, 82, 96
Idol, 5, 30; idolatry, 40
Idolaters, 33

Immanence, 25–28, 30
Incarnation, 3, 22, 24, 43, 54–55, 84
Inclusive Language Lectionary, 62–63, 66–67, 113 nn 28 and 24
Indians, 4, 76, 90
Inerrancy, 55, 62, 71
Infallibility, 60, 113 n 24
Injustice, 16, 19, 25, 40, 74, 89, 97
Inquisition, 91
Iran-contra hearings, 4
Israel, 13, 14, 57–58

Japan, 104 n 10
Jenkins, Ivor, 107 n 1
Jesus/Christ, 1, 3–4, 7–9, 11, 14, 18, 23–25, 27–28, 30–31, 51–52, 54–58, 61, 65–67, 69–72, 74, 77, 80–81, 84–85, 88, 91–95, 98–102, 104 n 7, 105–106 n 36, 108 n 16, 110 n 26, 111 n 5, 114 n 36; humanity of, 25, 55; suffering of, 47
John of Damascus, 12
Johnson, Barbara, 109 nn 10 and 14
Judas, 70
Judgment, 1, 3, 5, 27–28, 65, 101, 106 n 47
Jüngel, Eberhard, 50, 104 n 11, 110 nn 29–30, 111 nn 35 and 38, 115 n 13, 117 n 51, 118 nn 5 and 7, 119 n 24
Justice, 1–2, 15, 17, 22, 27, 29, 31, 33–34, 42, 44, 58, 64, 69, 72, 74, 82, 85–88, 90–91, 98, 108 n 22, 117 n 58; human; 8, 19, 22, 60; of God, 4–5, 8–9, 15, 19, 22, 29, 85
Justification, 8, 75, 82, 86, 91; justified, 100–101

Kairos, 97; *Document*, 85–86
Kant, Immanuel, 7, 18, 35, 105 n 20, 107 n 3
Käsemann, Ernst, 56, 111 n 10
Kaufman, Gordon, 9–10, 20, 24, 73, 105 n 30, 107 n 11
kenosis, 24, 55; kenotic theory, 108 n 22
King, Martin Luther, 82, 87
Kingdom, 58, 65, 74, 81; of God, 47, 74
Knowledge, 34, 37, 39–40, 47–48, 50, 56, 76, 92, 100, 105 n 17; of God, 6, 8, 39, 50, 61, 110 n 26
Koinonia, 107 n 1, 107 n 2
Koreans, 104 n 10
Küng, Hans, 79

Kuyper, Abraham, 75–76, 115 n 20

Labor, 4, 75, 82, 99
Laissez faire capitalism, 2, 69
Language, 10, 41–43, 48, 51–52, 54, 60,
    62–63, 65, 67, 78, 109 nn 9–10; about
    God, 8, 36–38, 42, 44, 80; biblical, 55;
    inclusive, 79
Latin America, 2, 64, 97, 108 n 16
Law, 8, 28, 57, 89, 91, 96, 98, 100–102
Lectionary, 62, 67, 113 n 35
Lehmann, Paul, 62; 67; 89; 91; 98; 113
    n 29; 114 nn 40 and 49; 115 n 3; 118
    nn 1, 8 and 22.
Leith, John H., 112 n 13
Lesbianism, 80
Liberalism, 7, 112 n 24, 113 n 24
Liberty, 9, 32–33, 74, 92, 94, 99, 101–103
Life, 3, 6, 7, 13–16, 20, 23, 26–27, 29–30,
    44, 48, 74–76, 84–85, 88, 91, 94–95,
    99–102, 119 n 27; human, 6, 26, 29–
    30, 54, 57–58, 85, 93, 102
Literalism, 62–63, 113 n 36, 114 n 36;
    literalists, 113 n 30
Liturgy, 73, 80
Livingston, James C., 105 nn 19 and 21
Logic, 49, 61
Logical positivism, 40
Logocentrism, 40
Logos, 30, 54, 58
Lord, 3, 15, 32, 37, 49, 55, 58, 62, 64, 66,
    84, 94, 100
Lord's Prayer, 105–106 n 36
Love, 9, 15–16, 18, 22, 28, 30, 42, 69, 86,
    89, 91, 95, 106 n 47; God's, 14–16, 19;
    human, 14–15, 19
Lordship, 24, 84, 99–100
Luther, Martin, 8–9, 14, 54, 65, 78, 82,
    85, 96, 105 n 24, 106 n 47, 111 n 4,
    116 n 34, 117 n 56, 118 n 20

Magna Carta, 60
Male, 4, 11, 65, 67, 80; oppression, 26;
    prejudice, 73; maleness, 66
Mamelodi, 17, 107 n 2
Man, 2, 7–8, 11, 25, 37, 39, 42, 51, 55,
    58, 64–65, 74, 81, 86, 92, 98, 100–101,
    105 n 16, 106 n 45, 112 n 12; spirit of,
    8; old, 92, 95
Mandela, Nelson, 107 n 1
Marduk, 108 n 13
Marquadt, Friedrich-Wilhelm, 47,
    110 n 29

Marx, Karl, 10, 88
Marxism, 25; -Leninism, 2, 60, 82;
    Marxist analysis, 10, 97
McFague, Sallie, 15, 106 n 49
McKelway, Alexander J., 108 n 25,
    117 n 49
Mercy, 63, 82, 95, 102
Merton, Thomas, 29, 1088 24
Messianism, 90
Metacritical, 39, 43, 46, 48, 50; move-
    ment, 11, 38–40, 43–44, 46, 50; self–
    correction, 65; reflexivity, 100
Meta-criticism, 37, 47
meta-noein/metanoia, 38, 46
Metaphor, 66, 111 n 5, 113 n 30
Metaphysics, 33, 42; Western 41;
    metaphysical, 35, 40, 42, 45;
Miami, 90
Middle Ages, 29
Middle class, 97
Migliore, Daniel L., 81, 104 n 3, 116
    n 42, 117 n 47
Miller, J. Hillis, 41
Miller, Patrick, 14, 106 n 46, 116 n 38
Minear, Paul, 63
Minister, 91, 116 n 27, ministry, 84,
    101, 114 n 26
Miracle, 28, 39, 55
Mirror, 55, 111 n 5
Misogyny, 85
Mollenkott, Virginia, 66
Moltmann, Jürgen, 46, 91, 110 n 28,
    118 n 9
Monarchy, 64
Monism, 107 n 13, 108 n 15,
Moral Majority, 105 n 33
Morals, 112 n 24
Mosaic stories, 58
Moses, 13, 37, 66
Mother, 28, 62, 67
Mount Sinai, 28
Mystery, 3, 6, 11, 31, 39, 51, 92, 94, 96

Narcissism, 80
National Council of Churches, 62
Nationalism, 73–74, 97
Natural order, 28
Nature, 6, 28, 69, 75, 91, 96; mysticism,
    80
Naudé, Beyers, 86, 107 n 1
Nazareth, 31
Nelkin, Dorothy, 75, 115 n 16
Neo-Protestantism, 106 n 45

Nestorius, 22
New Testament, 37, 58, 62, 65, 67
Newtonian laws, 112 n 24
Nicholas of Cusa, 6–7, 105 n 17
Niebuhr, Reinhold, 19, 82, 89–90, 107 n 7, 117 nn 55 and 1, 118 n 2
Nietzsche, 43–44, 78, 88
Nicaragua, 4, 27, 90
Nihilism, 29, 43
Nominalism, 8, 34, 36
nomos, 34
North, Oliver, 4
North America, 4, 59
North Carolina, 79
Nova Scotia, 90
Nuclear, age, 9–10; annihilation, 20

Obedience, 30–31, 52, 72, 73, 82, 90, 95, 99–102, 116 n 34
Odom, John, 116 n 32
Old Testament, 12, 37, 56–57, 65, 111 n 5
Ontario, 90
Ontology, 45, 48
Oppression, 2, 10, 13, 16–17, 22, 25–26, 29, 31, 58, 68, 71, 79, 83, 85, 87, 89–90, 96, 101, 117 n 58; oppressed, 1, 4, 15, 32–33, 44, 59, 70–72, 81, 85–86, 97, 99, 101, 104 n 10; oppressor, 4, 44, 101, 117 n 58
Orthodoxy, 7
Otto, Rudolf, 76
Overbeck, Franz, 83

Paradox, 117 n 58
Parricide, 41
Pascal, R., 118 n 20
Patriarchy 62, 87, 100
Patterson, Paige, 79
Paul, 37–38, 59
Peace, 1–2, 17, 58, 60, 64, 73–74, 83, 88, 92, 98, 117 n 58
Peale, Norman Vincent, 116 n 27
Peasants' Revolt, 96, 97
perestroika, 83
Person, 3, 11, 13, 18, 25, 34–35, 37, 44, 65, 95, 106 n 45
Pharisees, 66–67
Phenomena/phenomenology, 34–35, 77
Philosophy, 34–35, 38–42, 49, 61, 75–76, 84–85, 112 n 24, 118 n 22; Greek, 40; modern, 40

Phonic substance, 109 n 9
Physics, 93
Pietism, 7
Plaskow, Judith, 104 n 9
Plato, 34, 50
Platonic realism, 40
Plotinus, 6 108 n 14
Pluriformity, 75
Poles, 59
Politics, 71, 73–74, 98; right-wing, 79
Pontius Pilate, 95
Poor, 1–2, 4, 15, 29, 32, 59, 85–86, 101; poverty, 13, 69, 29, 44
Post, modern, 43, 77–78; existential, 78; historical, 78; liberal, 78; orthodox, 78; romantic, 78; theological, 78
Power, 1, 8, 19–20, 23, 25–26, 29, 39, 42, 45, 53, 55, 58, 59, 64, 67, 80, 86, 88, 90–91, 93, 95, 99, 102, 112 n 12; of God, 7, 19, 20, 22, 29, 47, 54, 58, 63–64, 70–71, 76, 85, 103
Prabhu, Joseph, 78, 116 n 30
Practical reason, 7, 36
Praxis, 58, 71, 74, 91, 96, 97, 115 n 2
Prayer, 26, 28, 49
Presbyterian, 72, 105 nn 26 and 33; General Assembly, 117 n 53
Presbytery, 117 n 58; of San Gabriel, 84, 117 n 53
Pretoria, 17
Pre-understanding, 10
Pride, 65, 67, 87, 91, 98
Priesthood, 73
Princeton Theological Seminary, 78, 106 n 46, 112 n 24
Prophets, 55, 58
Protestant faith, 15
Protestantism, 73, 97
Providence, 29, 61, 75, 108 n 15
Pseudo-Dionysius, 5–6, 110 n 26
Psychology, 76

Quayle, Dan 83
Quietism, Christian, 15

Race, 75, 82, racism, 2, 29, 60, 85, 97
Racial, equality, 69, 82; prejudice, 25
Rapists, 81
Rationalism, 113 n 24
Reason, 112 n 24
Red Guards, 64
reductio ad absurdum, 116 n 44
Religion, 7, 10, 45, 58, 77, 84; civil 73

Resurrection, 23, 39, 84–85, 119 n 27; of
    the dead, 47
Revelation, 6, 12, 18, 30–31, 34, 36, 43,
    47–48, 51, 55, 57–58, 62, 67, 70,
    73–74, 91, 110 n 26, 111 n 5
Revolution/revolutionary, 17, 22, 25–
    27, 29, 31, 47, 58, 74, 88–91, 96–102,
    110 n 29, 118 n 22; American, 27, 90;
    French, 27, 90
Ricoeur, Paul, 62–63, 94, 114 n 36,
    118 n 14
Righteousness, 87; of God, 8, 85–86;
    alien, 85
Ritschl, Albrecht, 8, 105 n 23
Roberts, Oral, 4
Roman magisterium, 79
Romania, 2, 5
Rome, 59
Romero, Oscar, 87
Ruether, Rosemary, 4, 56, 73, 80–81,
    112 n 11, 116 n 39, 117 n 48
Russell, Letty, 53, 101, 111 n 2,
    119 n 26
Russia, 2
Russian Revolution, 90

Sacraments, 39
Sacrifice, 25, 55
Salvation, 15, 55, 63, 118 n 14
Sarah, 58, 63, 65, 67
Saussure, 109 n 9
Scharlemann, Robert P., 33, 38, 45–46,
    109 n 1, 110 nn 24–25 and 27–28
Schleiermacher, Friedrich, 7, 105 n 18,
    115 n 24
Schnur, Susan, 73, 115 n 8
Scholastics, 33, schoolmen, 13
Scholder, Klaus, 115 n 12
Schuller, Robert H., 116 n 27
Science, 6, 34, 75, 77
Scottish, Presbyterianism, 112 n 12;
    Realism, 61, 112 n 24
Scripture, 12, 28–29, 36, 46, 54–55, 57,
    59–61, 64–66, 72, 79, 111 n 5, 112
    n 12, 113 n 35, 114 n 38; self-
    authentication of, 56
Searle, John, 40, 43, 109 nn 7 and
    12–13, 114 n 39
Second Helvetic Confession, 57
Seeberg, Reinhold, 104 nn 12 and 14
Segundo, Juan Luis, 10
Self, 19, 42–45, 84, 87, 89, 99, 115 n 24;
    projection, 6, 17, 25; negation, 6, 58;

abstraction, 8; critical, 10, 36–37, 58,
    66; consciousness, 7, 27, 29, 112–
    113 n 24; acceptance, 29; denial, 29;
    understanding, 31, 39, 44; revela-
    tion, 31, 36; disclosure, 11, 48, 50;
    bondage, 94, 96; enslavement, 94–
    96, 118 n 14
Serpent, 93
Seville, 91
Sex, 63, 81–82, 117 n 48
Sexism, 2, 29, 60
Sexual, consciousness, 73; oppression,
    73; exploitation, 80
Sexuality, 106 n 45
Shintoism, 108 n 13
Sign, 109 n 9
Silesius, Angelicus, 106 n 43
Similes, 66
simul justus et peccator, 117 n 58
Sin, 9, 23, 31, 37–38, 58, 85–86, 100,
    117 n 58
Skepticism, 36, 40, 112n 24
Slavery, 94, 100
Smith, Ellen and Nico, 17, 107 n 2
Sobrino, Jon, 59, 108 n 16, 112 n 18
Socialism, 29, 47, 83, 99, 108 n 25;
    religious, 47; national, 97
Sociology, 76
Soelle, Dorothy, 73, 115 n 10
Solipsism, 35
Son, 11, 13, 15, 24. 30, 54, 66–67, 74, 82,
    84, 94, 102, 105 n 26, 106 n 35
Sonship, 105 n 36
Soul, 118 n 20
Southeastern Baptist Seminary, 79
South Africa, 2, 17, 59, 69, 71, 75, 86,
    97–98, 107 n 2
South African Council of Churches,
    1
South America, 59, 69
Sovereignty, 99
Soviet Union, 5, 29, 69, 82–83, 92–93,
    98
Space, 35, 42, 95
Spirit, 108 n 23; of human beings, 7–8,
    43, 72; of God, 8, 11, 13, 15, 32, 54,
    56–57, 61, 84, 102; the internal testi-
    mony of, 57
State, 26, 64, 75, 85–86
Stoker, H. G., 76
Supernationalism, 6
Superstition, 112 n 12
supplements, 109 n 12

Taylor, Mark C., 43–44, 78, 110 n 20
Taylor, Nathaniel, 112 n 24
Temptation, 82, 93–94
Temple, 58, 65, 94
Tenure, 81
Terrible decree, 24, 79
Textual criticism, 114 n 36
Textuality, 43
Theism, 6, 61
Theology, 1–3, 5–13, 15, 23, 40, 42, 45,
    47–50, 54, 68–86, 89, 96, 102, 105 nn
    31–32, 110 n 29, 115 n 24; liberation,
    2, 4, 22–23, 25–27, 59–60, 71, 79, 97,
    104 n 10, 108 n 16, 114 nn 36 and 2;
    negative, 6, 7, 49, 110 n 26; imman-
    entist, 23–24, a, 43, 78; liberal 47;
    natural, 50; Medieval, 50; feminist,
    59, 106 n 46; political 59, 73–74;
    armchair, 71; of play, 71; of the
    goddess, 71; of the death of God, 71;
    professional, 71; pastoral, 71; popu-
    lar, 71; narrative, 77; American 77,
    97, 112 n 24; state, 86; process, 100
Theonomy, 101
Thieme, Robert Jr., 83
Thinking/thought, 12, 23, 33–41, 43,
    45–51, 48, 50–53, 57, 71, 75, 78,
    82–83, 94; about God, 10–11, 37–38,
    44–47, 49–51; about God as God, 35,
    47; *apophatic*,, 37; *theophantic*, 37; after
    (*metanoein*), 38, 100; authentic, 39,
    46–48; objective, 45; reflexive, 45–46;
    donative, 45; assertive;, 45; Onto-
    and Theo-logical, 45
Thomism, 8, 82
Tiamat, 108 n 13
Tiananmen Square, 64
Tillich, Paul, 5–6; 11–13; 18–19; 25–26;
    45; 57–58; 78; 81; 88–89; 97; 104 nn 7,
    12, and 13; 105 n 35; 106 nn 39 and
    44; 108 n 20; 112 n 16; 116 n 28;
    118 n 1
Time, 35, 42, 95
Torah, 58
Tories, 90
Totalitarianism, 94
Trace, 41, 43–44
Tracy, David, 78, 116 n 28
Tragedy, 86, 93, 97
Transcendence, 1, 3, 5, 8, 11, 13, 16, 24,
    30, 34, 40, 43, 44
Transfiguration, 91, 98, 118 n 22
Trible, Phyllis, 65, 79

Trinity, 11, 13, 31, 67, 84
Troeltsch, Earnest, 76
Truth, 2, 23, 34–35, 37, 39–45, 51–52,
    54, 56, 62, 67, 69, 79, 92, 112 n 12,
    113 n 24
Tutu, Desmond, 86
Tyranny, 95, 115 n 3

Uganda, 90
United Nations, 83
United States, 2, 17, 59, 62, 78, 83,
    107 n 2; Constitution, 60, 90
University of Tübingen, 79
Univocity, 62
Updike, John, 118 n 3
Utopia, 88; Marxist, 47, utopianism,
    93

via negativa, 7, 110 n 26
Virgin, 24
Vatican, 79
Vietnam, 97
Villa-Vicencio, Charles, 71, 115 n 3
Violence, 24, 27, 30, 56, 60, 86, 90, 97,
    107 n 1
Vocation, 70, 72–73, 82, 94
Volk, 74–75
Von Kircshbaum, Fraulein, 71
Von Rad, Gerhard, 106 nn 41 and 46
Voskuil, Dennis, 116 n 27

War, 17, 97
Warfield, B. B., 60–62, 72, 112
    n 21–23
Welch, Claude, 76, 115 n 24
Welfare system, 83
Wells, David, F., 116 n 33
Westminster Confession, 57
Whitehead, A. N. 20, 23, 207 n 9
Will, 13, 94–95; of God 2, 10, 14, 18, 20,
    24, 26, 28, 30–31, 55, 58, 70, 82, 88,
    90, 96–97, 101; human, 5
William of Occam, 34
Willis, E. David, 84, 117 n 54
Witherspoon, John, 112 n 24
Witness, 42, 53, 55–57, 60, 63–66, 72,
    88–89; biblical, 21, 38, 57
Woman 2, 4, 11, 25, 27, 29, 56, 62, 66,
    73, 77, 80, 86, 90, 92, 97, 100, 101;
    ministers, 73, *Women-Church*, 73, 80;
    women's church, 80; liberation, 63
World Council of Churches, 83

Word, 54–54, 56, 63, 72, 89, 110 n 20,
    111 n 5; of God, 10, 29, 51, 53–54,
    58–65, 72–73, 75–76; made flesh, 1,
    23, 51, 54
Working classes, 97
Worship, 1, 78, 80, 94; goddess,
    80

Writing, 40–44, 60, 71, 77, 109 n 12

Xenophanes, 109 n 4

Yahweh, 12, 14; Yahwist narrative, 24

Zoroastrianism, 77